POT-BELLIED PET PIGS
MINI-PIG CARE AND TRAINING

BY
KAYLA MULL
AND
LORRIE BLACKBURN, D.V.M.
aka LORRIE BOLDRICK, D.V.M.

All Publi
Orange, (
1989

Published by: All Publishing Company
2387 N. Flanders St.
Orange, CA 92865

Library of Congress Catalog Card Number: 89-86044

Publishers Cataloge in Publication Data
Mull, Kayla
Pot-Bellied Pet Pigs: Mini-Pig Care and Training.
by Kayla Mull and Lorrie Blackburn, D.V.M. --1st ed.
  p. cm..
  Mull, Kayla
  I. Animal Training - swine
  2. Pets - swine
  3. Swine - breeds, Pot-bellied Pigs
  4. Veterinary Medicine - miniature swine
I Blackburn, Lorrie joint author.
II. Title
SF 393 M85 1989   ISBN 0-962453 1 -0-2
636.4'85--dc 20

This book is dedicated to Walker;
a special friend who had lots of self-confidence and
a quirky sense of humor. I learned to respect and
enjoy his individuality.

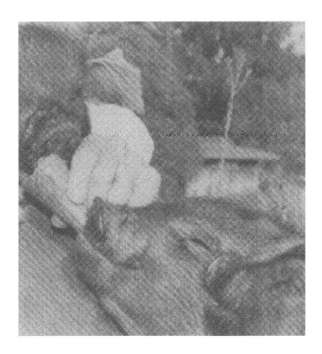

Pig for all ages
Photo by Lee Wood

Contents

Hogs and kisses
Photo by George A. Reynolds

Pigs on a Blanket
Photo by Heather Kingdon

ACKNOWLEDGMENTS

My deepest gratitude goes to the wonderful pigs
and people who have helped me through the writing
of this book. I am an animal person with more
experience communicating nonverbally with pigs
than with putting my thoughts on paper.

My special thanks to:

Katie Rigby for getting me started, so my scattered
instruction sheets became this book. She has a real
talent for organization, and her pig Casey is a
character.

Marjorie K. Diamond for making it all possible by
being my special friend and tireless supporter. She
and Jake Jacobs started this rolling and have helped
me over all the humps.

Lorrie, my thoughtful, inventive coauthor. It is the
nature of her profession that we first shared
problems and heartbreaks. In time, we were also
able to share all the joys of pig keeping.

Lorrie's family at Quillie Acres and my husband,
Marden, for their endless patience during rewrites
and rewrites and more rewrites. Marden is also the
liveware interface to "Hog-in-DOS," a mechanical
personality.

All of the people, who without hesitation, have graciously allowed me to bring my pigs for pictures in their swimming pools, yards, homes, and sometimes in their beds.

Once typed, these words were worked over by Jane Bryant, our wonderful editor and wordsmith. Her skills are quite remarkable. She quickly figured out that I talk with my hands and helped translate that to words on paper.

Finally, some of the individuals most deserving of my thanks won't read the book, but we hope they and their relatives will profit from it anyway. They are the pigs in our lives, some of whom shared our trials and errors. I love each of them very much. They are pigs in the best sense of the word and they appreciate being trained as such.

Among them are: Dr. Dolittle's Gub Gub, Piggy Sue, Hamlet's Sowliloquey, Cast Iron, Porkupine, China, Emperor Too Chins, Test Pattern, Mumbly Pig, Swine Romance, Lao Tsuie, Valenswine, Pigtails, Anna Mull, Frankinswine, Iggy, Tammy Fay Bacon, Sir Francis Bacon, Mr. Easy and so many other eccentric individuals that have been "Creatures of Comfort."

Kayla Mull, Norco, CA,1989

Learning confidence in crowds

Sit, Stay...Eat
Photo by Dr. Michael Boldrick

PREFACE

Many people today are interested in pigs as pets, but they can't find any information on either the care or training of pet pigs. The scarcity of information is due to the new arrival of the first pig breed that really stays the size of a dog--the Pot-Bellied pig.

The availability of miniature pigs suitable for use as pets has made it possible to develop a system to raise and train pigs so they become pets instead of pork. A small pig raised as a pig is only a pig; a small pig raised as a puppy is a pet.

A pet pig may be a young piglet, a weaner, a shoat or a sow. Pigs of all ages seem to learn pet ways easily as all are creatures that enjoy comfort. I have brought pigs into my home from newborns to adults with excellent results.

I consider a pig that is housebroken, comes when it is called, and that comes to me just to get a tummy rub a satisfactory pet. Most go far beyond that minimum friendship. I write about Pot-Bellied pigs, because I have the most experience with them.

This book is designed to be an owner's manual for raising and training a pet pig. It will help the pet pig owner care for his pig and prepare his pig to be a well trained pet. It is also written for people who love pigs whether or not they have ever owned, or ever plan to own one themselves. It can help you enjoy looking at pigs in a new way, just for the fun of it.

You cannot buy experience, you must earn it The next best alternative is to borrow it. With that intent, I will lend you my experience with pet pigs. Understand that I am still learning things the hard way myself. No two people and no two pigs act alike. Keeping that in mind, I offer the methods that worked for me. Hopefully they will be of some help to you.

When you complete this book you will not have a finished product, but you will be well on your way to enjoying your well trained and healthy pet pig.

PART ONE

BEGINNING WITH PET PIGS

Piglet meets grandchild
Photo by George A. Reynolds

INTRODUCING PET PIGS

Pigs in Legend

Noah is said to have created the pig to clean up the Ark. Storytellers say that Noah ran his hands over the body of the elephant and it gave birth to the first pig. From then on the pig's public relations image seems to have suffered. This is supposed to be due to the fact that pigs are home bodies and a poor choice for a nomadic tribe.

Pig Evolution

The story of the evolution of the pig is almost as fantastic. It begins 70 million years ago when the ancestors of the pig lived in trees. As time and generations passed they changed into huge Entelodonts. By the time the Entelodonts became extinct 40 million years ago there were three main pig-like dinosaurs. Palaeochoerus had tusks, and Listridon and Chaerotherium did not. In turn they too disappeared, only to be replaced by other pig-like creatures. About 25 million years ago small versions of modern pigs started to evolve. Originally there were two kinds of wild pigs, Asian and European, but after the Chinese wild boar became extinct all pigs were reclassified into one species.

All domestic animals trace back to wild ancestors. For Pot-Bellied pigs it is <u>Sus scrofa vittatus.</u>

Breed from the Orient

There is evidence, according to one source, that swine were domesticated before 6000 B.C. in Asia. These were probably Pot-Bellied pigs and they have remained almost unchanged since that time. Pot-Bellied pigs are considered to be the first domesticated breed of pig. The first book on pig raising was written in 3468 B.C. by the Emperor Fo-Hi of China.

Today there are more than 200 breeds of pigs in China alone. Most of these are large farm pigs, but some areminiature pigs. They are valued for the manure they produce, which is enough to help fertilize the family rice paddy. In addition, these "fertilizer factories" can reproduce themselves - or be eaten with the rice. Pigs do not require a lot of food to keep alive during lean times, so they make an excellent agricultural pig for small villages where people are close to starvation every winter.

Pigs in rural China are raised almost as second class children. They are fed at the table with scraps not good enough for children. They are bathed in bath water after it has been used on the children. They help warm the house with their body heat. Asian agricultural journals describe pigs as garbage disposals for fertilizing the fields. Yes, they are also eaten, usually for special festivals.

Pigs are highly regarded in Asia. The year of the pig comes every 12 years and is associated with prosperity. The most recent year of the pig was 1983. Each year pastries (filled with bean paste) made to look like cute Pot-Bellied piglets are an important part of Vietnamese children's festivals Brides are often given pig statues, not only r prosperity, but also because pigs are such good mothers.

History of Pet Pigs

Pigs in general have made excellent pets for centuries, but people have been reluctant to talk about them. In the United States, if I walk down any city street, I meet many people who have never even seen a pig up close. I also meet a few that quietly tell me about a pet pig they, or a relative, once raised. Every one who has had a pet pig is touched by their unique personalities. The major problem with pigs as pets has been the size and reputation of the pig. Pig owners have never organized and have not written books about pet pigs.

Trained pigs do have a history in the circus and in show business, but it is hard to say for sure if these pigs were pets. However, a lot of pig information did exist, but was kept secret because the trainers of these performing pigs wanted to earn a living, Tate most famous trained pig is Arnold Ziffel from the TV show "Green Acres." Actually, many pigs had that name as each outgrew the roll.

Farm piglets are often given as pets as gag gifts, usually with tragic results. These regular pigs, the kind that are supposed to become pork, get very large, making "pethood" a difficult venture. At three to five months old, they may weigh between 200 and 250 pounds. Adults of the same breeds may weigh 1200 to 1500 pounds. A few, dedicated "big" pet pig owners have pioneered methods of pig keeping, sometimes to the extent of reinforcing their houses to allow for their large pets. Unfortunately, most farm piglets do not fair well as pets.

Before Pot-Bellied pigs arrived in this country in 1985, miniature pigs were thought of as weighing 150 to 300 pounds. There are several breeds of laboratory pigs in various colors and structures. None of these breeds have become popular as pets.

Importation

One or more of the many different breeds of Chinese pigs were introduced into the western hemisphere from Asia by Columbus and other explorers. During pioneer times Chinese pigs were valued for their excessive fat. In modern times Chinese pigs are not normally imported directly from Asia because of certain diseases that are prevalent there. Because of the difficulty of importation, all of the Pot-Bellied pigs in the United States come from a very limited gene pool.

Pot-Bellied Pig Facts

Pot-Bellied pigs are truly exceptional. They are 1/10 the size of regular farm pigs, 1/3 the size of miniature horses! They are shorter than Labrador Retrievers and lighter in weight than Saint Bernards. They are larger than miniature poodles, in spite of some of the "hog wash" you may have read. Adult Pot-Bellied pigs usually weigh 70-150 lbs. Pot-Bellied piglets weigh 8 to 20 ounces at birth.

Pleasantly plump and gracefully sway-backed, Pot-Bellied pigs are charming, gentle, black pigs with short, wrinkled faces. They have softer bristles than most pigs. Hugging one is like hugging a hair brush. As pigs go, they are very exotic and attractive, yet primitive looking.

Their dispositions are excellent. Each is a confidently self-satisfied individual. When well cared for and raised with love, they are gentle, sweet tempered and seldom aggressive. They enjoy lots of attention and are swine and dandy pets. They are clean and smart. Pot-Bellied pigs, by nature, are calmer than regular pigs and squeal and root less than their farm cousins. Pigs are also one of the cleanest animals. They do not smell unless they are kept in a dirty pen or are terrified. Breeding males do have an offensive odor.

These less-than-knee-high pigs are special, people oriented pets. They are unusual pets for unusual people.

Collector Pigs

Pigophilia has many loyal fans. There are stores just selling pig things to a hog hungry public.
There is a book about "Porkabilia." The Mansion Hotel in San Francisco has a player pig-iano and several famous pig sculptures. The hates collection also includes stuffed pig toys, glass pig figurines, and other pig related items.

Pig books for adults are scarce, but there are excellent ones for children. My favorites are "Babe the Gallant Pig", "Pigling Bland", "Pigs!", and "The Wonders of Pigs".

National Pig Day

National Pig Day occurs on March 1st in the United States. The stated purpose National Pig Day is "To accord to the pig it's rightful, though generally unrecognized, place as one of man's most intellectual and useful domesticated animals."

Pig Sayings

A pig in the parlor is still a pig.

You can't make a silk purse out of a sow's ear.

What can you expect from a pig other than a grunt.

He steals the pig, but gives away the feet for God's sake.

"Give not that which is holy unto the dogs, neither cast your pearls before swine, lest they trample them under their feet, and turn again and lacerate you." Holy Bible, Matthew 7:6.

"Animals are equal, but some animals are more equal than others." George Orwell. Animal Farm.

"In doing of aught let your wit bear a stroke. For buying or selling a pig in a poke." Thomas Tusser. Five Hundred Points of Good Husbandry, 1557.

To market, to market, to buy a fat pig. Home again, home again, jiggity-jig.

'Just about as much right', said the duchess, `as pigs have to fly.'" Lewis Carrol. Alice's Adventures in Wonderland.

Never try to teach a pig to sing, it annoys the pig and wastes your time.

"Dogs look up to us. Cats look down on us. Pigs treat us as equals." Sir Winston Churchill, 1946.

POT-BELLIED PIGS

"Loud crys, but little wool, said the Devil when he sheared his hogs" From my great, great grandfather's diary 1879.

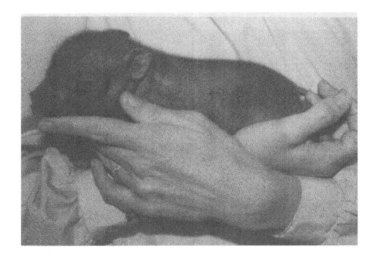

Pig in the hand

Home again, Jiggity-Jig

BEFORE YOU GET YOUR PIG

Special Needs for Special Pets

Special pets rarely fit ready made items. Be prepared
to special order things that you need for them. Pigs do
not fit dog harnesses and should not be fed dog food.
They love dog beds though and are more likely to
sleep in one than is the dog.

Ordering Pig Food

Special pigs need special pig food. See the Chapter
on feeding for the specific food for your age pig.
Don't just feed the pig pellets that are made for market pigs.

Dealing with Feed Dealers

Some dealers will try to tell you that a different food
is just as good as what we recommend. It probably is
not. Miniature pigs need a higher level of nutrients
per pound of food than is provided for farm pigs. We
are looking for the best nutrition possible in a feed,
not the cheapest way to squeak by. The protein level
in the foods we recommend is not too high. It does
not make pigs nervous or sick. Remember, as your
pig grows, he eats more feed and more hay which

automatically dilutes the protein level. Low protein is more dangerous than high protein in a diet.

Housebreaking Preparation

Be ready before your pig comes home. When your little friend arrives, his mother will already have him well on his way to being housebroken, so don't confuse him by leaving him where he is not supposed to mess. If he is young he will need to eliminate often. You may need to take him out five or six times a day.

Prepare a small pen outdoors. Then you can let him out without having problems finding him at night or with getting him back inside. If you are not able to let your piglet outside at least every four hours during the day, you might consider a piggy litter box. (See the section on Housebreaking in Chapter 15 for additional details on housebreaking in general.)

Companionship

Your piglet has rarely been alone and likes to be talked to. Plan to stay home with him the day he arrives. Let's face it, if you have to ask the boss for a day off to get acquainted with your new pig, he will have to give you some points for originality!

TO BUY A FINE PIG

Customer Support

The person you buy your pig from should be chosen both for his knowledge of Pot-Bellied pigs and for his attitude toward his pigs.

Customer support is a very important aspect of buying a pig. Prior to buying your pig, the breeder should be able to answer your questions. Beware of the breeder who is unable to answer your questions or the one who only tells you what you want to hear. If it sounds too good to be true, it probably is. There are pros and cons to owning pigs or any other pet. Once you have purchased your pig,

Your breeder should continue to support you. We all have a lot to learn about pet pigs, but that does not mean that we each must learn everything the hard way.

Disposition

The attitude of the breeder towards his pigs will be reflected in the disposition of your piglet. The breeder should respect a piglets feelings. He should be willing to stop to calm them if they do get frightened. This type of breeder is most likely to raise tame pet pigs.

Almost all weaning age piglets are "jumpy" and over-react to tactile and visual stimuli. Even sharp noises cause overreaction. But the piglet with the proper pet pig disposition immediately relaxes and comes back to see what startled him. A piglet that is only tame enough to hand feed is not house pet tame.

Choosing a Healthy Pet

Health is very important because only a healthy pet can be a joy to own. Health cannot be guaranteed. Healthy piglets come from healthy parents in a healthy herd, where preventive medicine is practiced on all animals. The breeder who works closely with his veterinarian probably keeps the healthiest herd.

Don't buy a sickly piglet just to save it. Feel sorry for yourself before feeling sorry for him. Choose a piglet that looks "healthy" to you. Your best bet is to have a veterinary health exam done on the piglet prior to purchase.

How Old for a Pet Piglet

Piglets are ideally weaned at 7-8 weeks of age. Early weaning and bottle feeding may result in malnour-ished piglets. The stress of weaning can be minimized for the piglet by spending his first week away from his mother on his home farm.

Homes where people are gone all day long should consider older piglets (3 months +) because younger piglets require more frequent attention for housebreaking, feeding, and proper mental adjustment.

Genetics

The current gene pool for Pot-Bellied pigs in the United States is extremely limited. Breeding stock should be selected carefully and genetic soundness should be considered. For most people,this is another situation where you have to trust your breeder and your veterinarian!

Size

Full grown Pot-Bellied pigs average 70-150 pounds in weight. The breed originated from a small wild pig and is healthy at this size.

Don't let size be the only consideration when choosing your pig. The Pot-Bellied pig is only 10% the size of a farm pig, so it is already truly a miniature pig. When people try to breed animals smaller, the animal becomes less healthy and genetically less sound. As pig breeders, we could learn from dog breeders who have inadvertently selected for health problems in their search for a smaller dog. Buyers encourage poor breeding techniques when they are interested in size alone.

Don't be misled by some of the sizes quoted for pet pigs. Adult weight is sometimes quoted for pigs at puberty, which in Pot-Bellied pigs is only three months of age. Some sellers tell you only part of the facts.

Boy or Girl

The choice is yours, but make it wisely with an eye to the future. Barrows and spayed females are the pick of the litter as housepets. Neutering is best done before you meet your piglet so you never have to worry. If you buy a piglet to have it spayed or castrated later, remember the risk is all yours.

Boars

Boars do not make good pets for many reasons. First, they have other priorities in their lives. In addition, a boar's breath and urine have a uniquely offensive odor. They foam at the mouth a great deal and the foam impregnates everything it touches. This odor is then difficult to wash off your hands, clothes, furniture, and even the walls.

Sows

Sows and gilts come in season every 21 days and are moody and noisy. Housebreaking is more difficult for an unspayed female. You will never be her number one priority even if she never has piglets of her own as her hormones keep reminding her of other interests. A sow is very protective of all piglets. She will never be the same sweet pet if she has a litter.

Barrows

Neutered male pigs are quieter, gentler, and friendlier than any-other kind of piglet. They lose little of their masculinity and remain decidedly boss hogs. They do not have the bad smell, difficult housebreaking, or unacceptable behavior of a boar.

Spayed Gilts

Spayed females remain feminine and are as easy going as barrows. They become quieter and housebreak more easily than unspayed females because they no longer have noisy, moody days.

Price and Value

Expect to pay a price for your miniature pet pig. All exotic livestock, including the more common miniature horses and llamas, are expensive. Miniature pigs are still fairly rare and are just now being recognized for their intelligence and suitability as house pets.

The price you pay for your pet pig represents an investment in your life and we recommend you purchase only from reputable breeders. The popularity of these little fellows has naturally spawned some "piggy" mills that raise their piglets in quantity, not quality. Check out your breeder and purchase with your head, not your heart.

STAYING OUT OF TROUBLE

Finding a Veterinarian

Find a veterinarian that is willing to learn. Farm-pig medicine alone is not good enough for pet pigs. The very best of pig medicine available to us today is designed to raise pork chops. Most market pigs are under 6 months old and breeding animals are retired at an early age. Pot-Bellied pigs are expected to live 12-18 years. They should be thought of as loved pets, not as pork chops. Minor and cosmetic problems that are of no concern in farm animals may be of great concern to Pot-Bellied pet owners

I prefer a veterinarian that takes care of wild animals and exotic pets. It is a matter of attitude. Exotic animal veterinarians are accustomed to new diagnostic and treatment challenges. It takes a lot of confidence to say to a stranger "I don't know." Our pigs need a veterinarian who keeps an open mind and is always willing to learn.

Use your veterinarian for routine matters so he can gain experience with your animals and with you.

Most problems, like cuts or scrapes, are not specifically pig problems. Then, if you are ever in big trouble, your vet will be willing to stick his neck out for you because you are no longer a stranger.

Avoid Dangers

Whenever possible, keep your pig safe by actively protecting him instead of just hoping that nothing will happen. Poison proof your home like you would for a child. Children and pigs may both play in the garage and garden where fertilizers and pesticides may be a problem. Mouse poison is made to taste good; antifreeze tastes good too. These chemicals can be deadly for your pig. Pigs are usually sensible about poisonous plants, except when they are bored, lonely, or locked in a pig pen. Make sure your pig's part of the yard is clear of any potentially harmful plants.

Swimming pools and spas are dangerous. Many pigs live around them without having problems, but even pigs that swim regularly with their owners could drown if they fall in the pool. If they are alone and panic, they won't necessarily be able to find the stairs Keep in mind that hot food or drinks can scald a pig. Alcohol, cigarettes, and chocolate are all potential poisons.

If you see a potentially dangerous situation in the making, do whatever you can to avoid it! If a problem does occur, try to find the cause of the problem and correct it.

HOME AGAIN, HOME AGAIN

Pigs 'N Wings

If your piglet is arriving by plane you should plan on getting to the airport before the plane is due to arrive. Freight or cargo offices can be hard to find! If your pig has been shipped "counter to counter," be aware that he will probably arrive at the baggage area.

Leave your piglet in his travel cage until you get home and can let him out in a safe area. Do not risk losing him in a strange and dangerous place. He has spent a long time in his crate; he can wait a little longer for a safe place to be let out.

You may want to have a few small pieces of fruit with you for your new pet. He may appreciate something juicy, like part of an apple or a few grapes, which fit between the bars of his crate.

Talk to your pig as soon as you get him. Pleasant sounding words or singing will usually quiet him if he is upset. You can be sure he has missed "conversation." Pigs normally keep up a steady patter of soft grunts that sound something akin to "un-huh" or quiet belly laughs.

When You Get Home

The piglet has had a very long trip and a nice nap while he traveled, but he is all alone in a strange place for the very first time. This is the time to minimize stress and to be there for him as an undemanding and non-judgmental friend.

You should let him out of his crate as soon as he is in his own safe place at home. His first exploration should be confined to the special pen you set up for him outside or a small enclosed space with all the doors closed like a bathroom, closet, or pantry, (If you take him outside first, it gives him a chance to relieve himself in the proper place and decreases the chances of him starting life in his new home with an "accident.") Sit quietly on the floor and let him explore. Eventually he will come to see who you are; give him a piece of food.

If you can't wait to see him, sit right in front of the crate door. Reach in but do not pull him out. He is a baby and his bones are still soft. Be gentle. Place your hand on his behind and he may jump out. If not, offer food or just sit quietly so he comes out to see you. Slowly put your hand under his chin and scratch between his front legs. Put your other hand under his rump leaving his legs alone. Lift up his chin and rump simultaneously. Keep him level. If he screams and struggles, put him back in his nice safe cage for a few seconds; it smells like home. Then you can start again.

Seventh inning stretch

FEEDING PIGS WITH GOOD TASTE NOT PIGS THAT TASTE GOOD:

Some kinds of pigs enjoy fine dining while other kinds will become part of a fine dinner. Pot- Bellied pigs are part of the former group and should be fed food designed for the small, but long lived pet pig.

Feed your pig properly in order for him to have the longest possible life expectancy. Many factors affecting the health of your pig are out of your control, but the diet is completely in your hands. Take advantage of it.

Kinds of Food

Pigs are not dogs, and dog food is not a balanced diet for a pig. Pigs are not calves, and calf manna is not an adequate diet. Don't feed these improper foods just because they are easily available and the proper pig food is not. If you need everything easy get the same kind of pet everyone else has.

Many pet pigs suffer from both malnutrition and obesity. Avoid food intended for market hogs. Regular pig feeds are designed as "least cost rations" for animals that eat large quantities, grow quickly, but live for only a few months. The vitamin and mineral content of these feeds are not adequate for our pets in the small quantities that they eat.

Mazuri markets a line of Mini-Pig feed. The Mini-Pig Youth (#5Z90) is for baby piglets from weaning to 4 months of age. Mini-Pig Active Adult (#5Z91) is for pigs from 4 months to 18 months of age. And Mini-Pig Elder (#5Z92) is for all average adult pigs.

The feeding directions on the bag would make most pigs very fat without exercise. For most pigs we feed 1% of body weight daily. The Mazuri feed is available in 25 pound bags for your convenience.

Your local Purina dealer can special order these feeds for you. Be good to your dealer, it is extra work for him also. It may take approximately two to eight weeks to arrive. Many feed stores do keep a stock of Mini-Pig feeds.

How Much to Feed

Pot-Bellied pigs tend to gain weight quite easily and must be fed carefully rationed amounts of food. A young piglet eats approximately one half cup of feed per 20-25 pounds of piglet per day. Make him "work" for his food; don't just put it in a dish and leave, unless he is already perfect and does everything you want him to do.

Increase his food intake slowly as he grows so he does not get too fat or too thin. The recom- mended amount is too much for some pigs and some unusually active pigs need a bit more when they get limited pasture or no other extra food.

For older pigs feed approximately one cup of food per 60-95 pounds of pig. It is preferable to split this into two feedings per day, even in adult pigs.

Pasture

Along with his special pig food, your pig needs to graze in your yard, or to eat some hay. He does not need to look like a balloon belly or tear up your yard.

There are no magic numbers as far as amounts of this type of food that your pig should eat. Use common sense to balance the amount of roughage with the specified amount of pig food he gets daily. In most cases, you do not need to restrict your pig's grazing. However, if your yard is large and provides too much fattening food (that is, your pig is getting fat!), keep him inside for part of the day. On the other hand, if your yard is small and/or there is no hay available, extra veggies are especially important since he does need some roughage.

Remember that even if you are able to provide your pig with all the essential nutrient requirements in one cup of pig food a day, he may think he is starving. It doesn't take long to eat that one cup. The extra roughage gives his mouth something to do and adds only a few calories to his diet. Adult pigs should also receive

100-200 IU of Vitamin E per 60-100 pounds of pig each day.

Treats

Pigs must be fed treats with care. Your pig will eat almost anything you offer him. It is up to you to limit your treats to healthy foods. Cookies and candy are empty calories to pigs as well as humans. Try using unsweetened raisins (not chocolate or yogurt coated) or diced fruit bits as treats. Carry some in your pocket at all times and always be ready to reward your pet when he does what you ask. A single raisin along with a word of praise can make your pig happy and proud of pleasing you. Remember to use the raisin and praise frequently. Juicy treats like melon and grapes are fun and messy. They are also a good way to increase your pig's water intake. Always remember to watch the calories, and do not feed so many treats that you are tempted to feed less of his regular pig food. He needs that daily ration to fulfill his vitamin and nutritional requirements.

Growth

The Pig Weight Chart is a compilation of the age and weight of many Pot-Bellied pigs of all sexes, both under and overweight. Your pig will grow to his genetic potential in size. Proper feeding can get him there at the right weight and-in the right length of time.

Pig Weight Chart

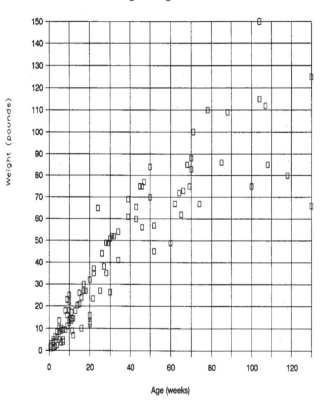

Small Pigs

Restricting feed may slow your pig's growth rate, but is not likely to affect his ultimate size. Even if he is restricted enough to change his body structure, he will still pass his original, genetic size on to any offspring. Pot-Bellied pigs are already extremely small compared to domestic farm pigs.

If you try to stunt his growth you are likely to shorten his life expectancy due to malnutrition. Starving pigs into submission or smallness only ruins the breed and deprives you of a healthy pet.
Enjoy your Pot-Bellied pig as he was meant to be; don't try to shrink him into something he isn't.

Fat Hogs

At the other end of the scale, overfeeding is also to be avoided. Excess feed does not create a larger pig, only a fatter one. If you wanted a larger pig, you would have chosen a farm breed rather than a Pot-Bellied pig. Obesity can create serious health problems and may kill many fine pigs.

Dieting

A continuously controlled diet is the best means of weight control. It is always best not to let your pig get too fat, but things sneak up on us all. If your pig does get overweight, you should gradually reduce the excess weight. Avoid fad diets and crash diets. Keep a watch over his ribs, shoulders, back-bone and hips. If you can't feel all of them, he is too fat. If you can easily see these same bones without feeling, then he is probably too thin. (Hint: the wrinkles on his sides are not ribs if he feels like the Pillsbury Dough Boy.)

For best dieting results, slowly decrease his calories. First cut back on fattening treats. Check with all friends and family to see if he is pigging outon any empty calories. Next restrict his extra food; even hay and grass can be fattening. Encourage him to drink more liquids ("Weight Watchers" recommends this). Do not just stop feeding him. He needs protein and vitamins to burn calories and lose weight safely. By carefully controlling his intake of pig food you can keep him in prime condition.

"You Are What You Eat"

Pig food alone is not balanced and adequate for our miniature pigs. Vitamins are not a replacement for a balanced diet. Even a large pasture (unless, of course, you have access to a whole forest) is not a proper diet by itself. Your careful control of the pig food, rough-age, and vitamins offered to your pig will provide all the ingredients for his long and healthy life.

Water

Water should never be forgotten with any animal, and it is essential for pigs. Your house pig should have water available to drink at ALL times

He may be a very messy drinker, but you should accept this as part of being a good pig owner. Use a heavy crock water bowl that does not slide around and is difficult to tip over.

Pigs love to splash and blow bubbles in water. You might try placing the water bowl in your stall shower where the mess won't bother anyone. You could also try putting the water bowl on a towel or rug that soaks up the spilled water and is easily changed. Whatever you do, do NOT restrict the water.

Water should also be provided for your pig for soak-ing, cooling, playing, or cleaning. Pigs do not sweat and need external water on their bodies for proper cooling in hot weather. They much prefer clean water to mud, but take what they can get.

Two pigs in a tub

DETAILS OF PIG HOUSING

House and Garden Pigs

The joy of having a pet pig includes the whimsy of having a pig in the parlor. Pigs as house pets seem simple and practical to me. They are cleaner and fresher smelling than any dog I have ever known. They spend most of their time either searching for crumbs to eat or sleeping.

Like any other creature, pigs need the proper environment to be healthy and happy. This includes some outdoor space--even for the most contented of house pigs. After all pigs did not become world renowned truffle hunters while never digging in the flower beds or eating the flowers.

One of the prettiest sights at my house is Hamlet asleep on my feet as I type. He resembles a large, colorful foot pillow with a black background dotted with tiny yellow flower petals. a garden piggy, he has been outside eating wild mustard flowers before coming to warm my feet and keep me company as a house piggy.

Yard and Garden Pigs

Pigs kept outside full time, must be provided with shade and water during the day and insulated housing with warm, comfortable bedding at night. They also need plenty of space. The more space your pig has to explore the less bored he is likely to become. A happy comfortable pig will be less of a root hog.

If you are an outdoors kind of person, your pig will enjoy being an outdoors kind of pig. The greatest danger of keeping a pig outside full time is that a pig who is "out of sight, out of mind" may accidentally be neglected. Remember, you get out of a pig what you put into him.

Rooting in the garden is normal pig behavior. Some yards are tougher to damage than others; and, some owners are more tolerant than others. It is often in the garden that a pet pig seems most like a pig and not like a dog. The amount of re-landscaping done by a pig depends on how soft the soil is and how tempting the plants are. Acorns, like truffles, will be rooted up by pigs.

Dog runs can make good pig playrooms, if provided with shade and a soft nest. But they come uncomfortably close to being prisons. An imprisoned pig tends to be a boring pet.

Strong fences are needed to keep pigs safe and alive. Without good fencing the pig is at the mercy of every stray dog. At weaning age, he is especially vulnerable, but even when he grows up, some dogs and coyotes will still think he is fun to chase and to taste! Check the top of your fence to be sure that it will keep other creatures out. Check the bottom of the fence to make sure it will keep your piglet in. He won't dig out under a fence on purpose, but he may toot right next to a fence and end up with an escape route. Once loose, he may be tempted by the call of the wild.

Temperature

Pigs are very susceptible to heat and cold. Pigs moved during the heat of the day easily get heat stroke. A pet owner, especially a child, may not understand that his pet pig cannot play in the heat of the day. At the other extreme, he may be surprised that his pig tends to be grumpy if he is expected to get out of his bed when it is cold outside.

Temperature control is most important, in caring for your pig. Pigs originally developed in forests where they would build soft, warm nests in the fallen leaves and soak in cool, shady ponds. When we take pigs away from the forests, we become responsible for finding substitutes for these natural temperature controls. Your pig depends on you to provide him with the conditions he needs to stay warm or cool.

When a pig is cold he may tear his bedding. When he is hot he may spill his water as he attempts to find comfort. He may be troublesome as a pet if you neglect him.

The comfortable temperature for a pig is almost the same as for a human. Ideal temperature for adult pigs is 60 to 75 degrees F; for babies, it is 80 to 85 degrees. You can test the temperature in your pig's housing by sitting in it, in shirt sleeves, for an hour one night. Then, try exercising there in the heat of the afternoon. If you are not comfortable your pig will not be either. From a pigs point of view, uncomfortable can be unsafe.

Pools

Wading pools and shade are important for your pig to use to stay cool if the temperature gets over 70 or 80 degrees. A shady, shallow pool of clean water is ideal. A small, children's wading pool usually delights your pig. You will be equally delighted watching his antics in it. These pools are hard to find in the winter, but plastic snow sleds, plaster mixing troughs, and hog pans all make good bathtubs for different sizes of pigs. Let young piglets play in a water puddle on the patio or on the wet grass - though wet grass does encourage rooting.

Pigs are afraid of slipping and like to get into their pools very carefully. Don't be discouraged if your pig has to have privacy before using his pool. Don't force him into the water and don't splash him. It may take several days before he decides to take the plunge. If he continues to avoid the water, you may want to try another size pool.

Soaking in his pool is the most important way for your pig to stay cool. A happy, comfortable pig is less destructive and healthier.

Space

We do not know the ideal amount of space for a pig, but we do know that cramped quarters can strain a pigs legs by forcing him to twist when turning. Due to the pig's ever present weight problems his legs may be a weak point. Never leave a pig in a pen smaller than 4 feet by 12 feet. A longer and wider pen is better. A pig needs to walk and turn with ease. Large crates are good for house breaking but for living quarters the pig should have more turning room.

Floors

Whenever possible, the surface your pig walks on should be non-skid to minimize slipping, which strains the tendons. Indoor-outdoor carpet is a very good flooring especially when well padded. Concrete floors, on the other hand, lead to many different feet and leg problems because they are hard, cold, and slippery.

Bed

Your pig's bed should be well padded as hard sur-
faces can lead to arthritis in old age. His bed should
also include lots of blankets to keep him warm. He
will tear at his bedding if he does not feel he has
enough. Remember that his bed in the wild would be
an elaborate nest made in a pile of soft leaves under
the branches of a thick, low bush. In nature it would
also be padded with the fat, warm bodies of other
pigs

Zoning

Most zoning ordinances are based on large, farm-type
pigs that are often kept in smelly pens. These zoning
rules, which are subject to interpretation, vary greatly
from town to town and even between areas in the
same town. Some local governments are changing
their rules to allow pet pigs, but your town may not
have heard of miniature pet pigs yet. If you approach
them with tact and don't rush them, you have a
chance to get permission for your pig.

Recently in Ventura County, California, a miniature
horse named Ragtime was ruled by a judge   to be a
household pet, not livestock or a farm animal.

As long as only responsible pet owners make "the
news," zoning rules should get easier. When   some-
one makes trouble they may get tighter again.

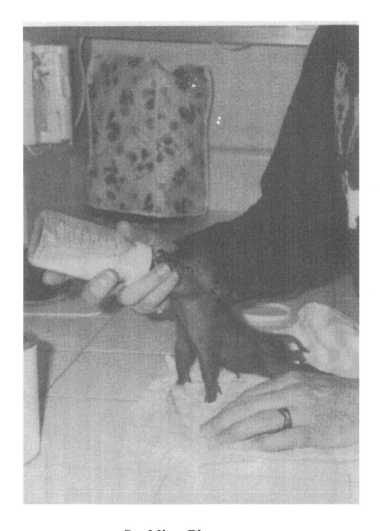

Suckling Pig
Photo by Allie Blackburn

Ready to be caught

PART TWO

HEALTH CONSIDERATIONS

Hollywood Hog
Photo courtesy of Chris Blackmore

PET PIG HUSBANDRY

How to Know the Normal Animal

Sick animals always seem to be most important to the owner. But, how do you know if your pig is sick? The good pig owner knows his healthy animal so well that any subtle change in behavior alerts him to the earliest signs of illness. He can then follow through with a more thorough evaluation of the animal's condition to decide if professional help or treatment is necessary.

The key is knowing your pig. I don't mean knowing the normal values of respiratory or pulse rates, although they are mentioned shortly. I mean knowing your pig's normal behavior patterns, attitudes, posture, etc. - and asking questions when anything seems out of the ordinary. If your pig usually knocks you down for his food and today he doesn't- why? If she is usually perfectly housebroken and today she isn't - why? If he is always beside you when you sit down to watch TV and today he is nowhere to be seen - why? These questions may all have answers that are unrelated to health problems, but the questions should come to mind with each and every pig owner. None of these situations should be ignored.

If the above questions don't have simple answers like "your daughter just fed the pig ten minutes earlier" or "she's in season," then you need to check the animal over carefully. First, stand back and observe. Are there any other signs you should notice? Is the pig coughing, straining, preferring to lie down, pacing, circling, etc? Is he shivering or is his hair coat "puffed" up? Check his stool, Is it firm, soft, or liquid diarrhea? Now put all your signs and symptoms together and either come up with a tentative diagnosis or call your veterinarian with the information.

By observing that your pig is less than 100% normal you may be able to take action to prevent a serious problem. By checking him out carefully and thoroughly you will be prepared to answer any questions your veterinarian may have if you find it necessary to contact her or him. It's far better to waste a few minutes of your time on a healthy pig who is just acting weird than to lose him because of inattention.

Your first awareness of abnormal behavior may be accidental. We've all gone about our business of the day, done our chores and then realized that "something wasn't right." In retrospect you realize that the pig's water dish was still full and he always spills it all over the kitchen floor. Pay attention when you get "vibes" that something is wrong. Follow through and find the source of the problem. Spend a little extra time each day just observing your pig. Sit with him for a quiet "study" time. It's fun and relaxing and you may notice something important.

The following values are considered "normal" for Pot-Bellied pigs. These figures may help you when you are trying to determine if your pig is sick.

Normal Pot-Bellied Pig Values

Rectal temperature	101-104° F
Pulse	70-110/min.
Respiration	20-30/min.
Puberty	2-4 months
Estrus cycle	19-25 days
Estrum	1-3 days
Gestation	106-113 days

Crossing State Lines

According to the USDA all pigs are livestock. There is no allowance made for pet pigs. Transportation of pigs is governed by very strict rules that differ from state to state. Before you plan to take your pet pig with you on vacation, check with your own state and all the states into which you may travel to find out what restrictions apply and what paper work is required. Many states require Pseudorabies (PRV) and Brucellosis (BRU) blood tests within 10 days of entrance into that state. Some states require an entry permit. Some states require that you repeat blood tests of your pig if you have left the state and then reentered. Most all states require a health certificate.

Even if you have never been stopped when crossing a state line in the past, don't take a chance on having your pig confiscated. Do all the blood testing and paperwork before and after you travel so you can all enjoy the trip.

POT-BELLIED PIGS

Remember, while you are traveling and while you are at home, to try to keep your pet pig isolated from other pigs, especially market animals. Many states, especially mid Western and Eastern, are having outbreaks of PRV. You don't want to risk exposure to this disease.

Leaping Lizzy
Photo by Heather Kingdon

VACCINATIONS

Disease Prevention

Pigs are susceptible to many diseases - some of which have vaccinations available, and some which don't. "An ounce of prevention is worth a pound of cure." This old adage is very meaningful. It is much easier to give your healthy pig two or three vaccinations a year than it is to treat your sick pig for even one disease. Unfortunately, no vaccine is perfect and a few animals contract diseases even if been vaccinated.

Many pig diseases are spread directly from pig to pig and your pet pig may never come in direct contact with another pig. At first glance it would seem wasteful to vaccinate such an isolated animal. But then stop to consider the nature of the pet pig owner. He avails himself of any opportunity to see other people's pigs. It's fun to visit with other pet pigowners and compare stories. It's even more fun to visit the "real" pigs at the county fair to remind yourself why you have a miniature pig as a pet. Pig "germs" can be carried on your clothes and hands. You can expose your pig to disease without him even having the pleasure of meeting the other pig!

So, until pet pigs have been around long enough to gather some statistical data on disease incidence, I strongly recommend vaccination. (We are NOT going to collect disease data on MY pet pig!)

Following is a list of some of the more common disease organisms for which there is a vaccine available, the diseases they usually cause in pigs, and finally the currently recommended vaccines.

Bordetella bronchiseptica: Pasturella multocida Type A; Pasteurella multocida Type D.

The combination of these three bacteria and their toxins causes a disease called Atrophic Rhinitis. Dust, poor ventilation, and unclean conditions also contribute to the progress of the disease. Atrophic Rhinitis causes the inside of the nose to grow incorrectly and the entire snout becomes twisted and shortened. It is unhealthy and unsightly.

Erysipelothrix rhusiopathiae.

This organism causes Erysipelas, a disease that can cause acute deaths or chronic arthritis and heart problems. It is especially a problem in younger animals.

Leptospirosis species

The Leptospirosis spirochetes cause the disease with the same name. Presently there are five types included in most vaccines, and a sixth is expected to be included soon. All the types cause the same clinical signs, but each requires separate vaccination. This disease causes kidney and reproductive problems and recovered animals are carriers of the disease organism. Lepto can cause disease in other animals and in humans.

Porcine Parvovirus

This virus causes reproductive problems in female pigs. It does not cause the severe disease with diarrhea and vomiting that is seen in dogs, and it is not contagious to dogs. Sows and gilts should be vaccinated prior to being bred because the virus can infect the unborn babies. Boars should also be vaccinated to prevent virus transfer in the semen.

Hemophilus pleuropneumoniae

This bacteria causes a respiratory disease of swine called Hemophilus pneumonia. Affected animals may die or be left with chronic lung problems.

Escherichia coli; Clostridium perfringens

These two organisms can work separately or in conjunction with one another to cause diarrhea.. Piglet diarrheas can be fatal in less that 24 hours in young piglets. Piglets can die of either of these infections without even exhibiting diarrhea.. Vaccinating a pregnant sow late in gestation helps protect piglets. Some breeders prefer to vaccinate newborn piglets individually. Pick the method that best suits your management, but DO vaccinate.

Pseudorabies (PRV) Virus

This organism causes Pseudorabies, which may also be called Aujeszeky's Disease. This is of great importance in the US. The USDA routinely tests hogs belonging to large breeders. Pigs which test positive are quarantined and are only allowed to leave the quarantine are after they are butchered. Some herds are tested quarterly and are certified free of the disease. The disease is caused by a herpes virus and there is a vaccine available.. However, certain states do not allow the use of the vaccine. Check on the rules of your state before considering vaccination. PRV can cause fatalities in very young piglets, but the disease is far less serious in older pigs. PRV will NOT affect humans, but can cause fatal disease in other domestic animals.

Rabies can occur in pigs, but there is no legal vaccine for use in the porcine species.

Vaccination Recommendations:

The vaccinations we are currently using are:

a. Suvaxyn PLE (Fort Dodge) - vaccine against Parvovirus, Leptospirosis and Erisipelothrix.

b. Rhinogen BPE (Intervet) - vaccine against Bordetella, Pasteurella Type A and Type D and Erisipelothrix.

All these vaccinations area 2cc dose and can be given subcutaneously. We have found the loose skin in the flank area to be an ideal place to give these vaccines. All pigs, young or old, are given an initial series of two doses 3-4 weeks apart followed by yearly boosters (one dose only). Breeding females may also need additional boosters.

We have chosen vaccines that cover the proper diseases, have small dose sizes, and can be given by the subcutaneous route. Most of these vaccines will leave a small lump under the skin that may persist for three to six weeks. These specific vaccine recommendations will change according to area of the country where the pig lives. Check with a veterinarian in your area to see which of these preventable diseases are a problem. There is no reason to vaccinate for a disease if your pig will never receive exposure.

NOTE: Beware that a pet pig can be far more difficult to restrain for vaccination than a farm or pen raised pig. A food reward immediately following the shot will end the experience on a positive note.

Piglet yawning

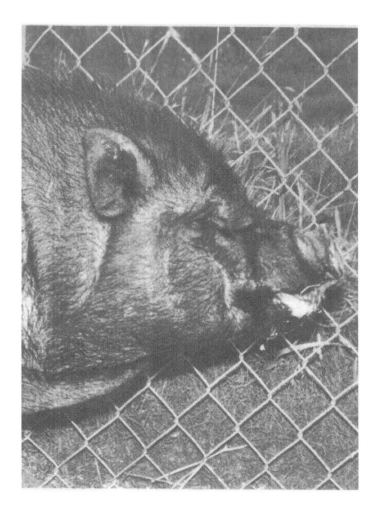

Boars normally froth at the mouth

PREVENTIVE MAINTENANCE

Hoof Care

Pigs need pedicures regularly. More exercise means less need for trimming, but he still needs some. Proper care of the pig's foot is a bit more difficult than the proper care of a dog's or horse's foot.

Dogs have a fairly well delineated nail with an obvious "quick" to be avoided when trimming. Horses have farriers to trim their hooves, saving the owner the need for training or purchase of equipment.

But pigs are another story. They don't like being restrained for foot handling; they require some special equipment; and neither dog groomers nor horse farriers have enough time or patience for good results. Regular dog nail clippers work fairly well on the pig's dewclaws, but a small pair of horse hoof nippers work better on the pig's hooves. Pruning shears and cable cutters also work. A hoof rasp or acrylic fingernail file can be used to smooth edges. Used frequently, the rasp can help keep the foot from needing other care.

The dewclaws need to be shortened and blunted. They also need to be filed and smoothed along the back or side edge. There are blood vessels and nerves in the dewclaw, so care must be taken not to clip off too much. Since these dewclaws are the nails that are most likely to hurt you as your pig steps or climbs on you, it is worth the time to do a careful job.

The primary hooves (toes) need to be shortened and blunted. Small slices of hoof should be nipped off at a time while you watch carefully for a thin pink line to appear just under the cut surface. Since the nerve extends farther into the hoof than the blood vessels, the pig will probably complain of pain just before you either see the pink line or actually cause bleeding. Quit when he complains! And quit even one slice sooner on the rest of that toe. If you do cause bleeding, apply some styptic powder. Pet stores sell "Blood-Stop" for dog's nails and; this works equally well on pigs.

If you learn to trim hooves carefully and without causing pain and bleeding, your pig can learn to tolerate the procedure. He will probably never like it and may always talk and complain while you are working on him. Avoid a screaming fight if you can. Using a second person to feed him while you trim may help. (Stop when he has eaten too much of his daily food allowance.)

A pig's hooves must be kept trimmed to prevent him from becoming crippled as he ages. Start while he is young and exercise as much patience and tolerance as you have to make this procedure acceptable to you both.

Teeth

Pigs have 28 baby teeth and 44 adult teeth. They are born with 8 sharp teeth called needle teeth. These teeth are usually trimmed short by the breeder to help protect both the sow's nipples and the other piglets from injury. The rest of the baby teeth erupt by 5 months of age. The baby teeth are then lost, and replaced by permanent teeth, between 8 and 20 months of age. Teething can be uncomfortable for your pig and you may hear him grinding his teeth occasionally during this time. If he is less than two years old and you see no signs of other problems, then you are probably safe to assume that he is teething.

Pot-bellied pigs tend to have their lower front teeth stick out farther than their upper front teeth. This condition is called an undershot bite and is normal for this breed.

Tusks teeth that continue to grow throughout the pig's life. The permanent tusks erupt at 10-15 months of age and develop in both male and female pigs. However, male hormone stimulates excessive growth of the tusks, so tusks grow much longer in boars than in barrows, gilts or sows. The upper tusk grows in a sideways and backward curve; the lower tusk grows out and backward. Both upper and lower tusks eventually protrude from the lips. The pig keeps the tusks sharp by grinding them together. These teeth can cause injury to the owner or to other animals. A nonvicious boar may just rub against you and catch his tusk in your pant leg. The resulting injury may be accidental, but it can still be quite serious.

To prevent injuries, either accidental or deliberate, the tusks should be trimmed on a regular basis. Boars probably need trimming every 6-18 months while barrows and females can last years between trimmings. Your veterinarian can trim the tusks with the pig under heavy tranquilization.

Eyes

Pot-Bellied pigs tend to have excess wrinkling on their faces. The wrinkles are cute but cause extra folds of skin around that sometimes allow the upper eyelid to roll in. This condition is called entropion. Severe cases of entropion require surgical correction. Mild cases, that are not irritating in young pigs, may disappear as the animal matures and "grows into his skin." Since entropion puts the hair on the outside of the eyelid in contact with the cornea, it is imperative that the condition not be ignored or permanent damage may be done to the animal's sight.

Entropion is relatively uncommon in Pot Bellied pigs. A more common problem, that is unique to Pot-Bellies, occurs when a few of the lateral lashes of the upper lid rest on the tear film over the cornea and become entrapped under the lower eyelid. This is not a true entropion because the lid is in the correct position on the eye. Since the lashes are floating on the tear film, there is no damage to the cornea and you may not even notice the problem unless you look for it carefully.

These aberrant eyelashes are highly unlikely to be the primary cause of eye discharge, but there is a tendency for all of us to blame them first. You may neglect a different and possibly more serious problem by assuming the lashes are the problem. However, if any other condition causes irritation of the cornea these floating lashes may aggravate the problem.

Many pigs develop an ugly, thick, brown discharge from the corners of their eyes. This can easily be cleaned off if it is first softened with a wet washcloth or a bland eye ointment. Don't try to just pick it off or the skin underneath will become irritated. The skin may also be irritated if the discharge is not removed. In addition, the pig may do more damage by scratching the side of his face on fences or furniture in an attempt to relieve the irritation. The discharge often disappears if the pig is given Vitamin E at a dose of 100 - 200 IU per day per adult pig (60 - 100 pounds).

Skin

A baby pig's skin and haircoat is soft and a pleasure to touch. An adult's skin becomes quite thick and the haircoat becomes sparse and bristly. This is normal for our pigs and we, as pig owners, should be willing to accept it.

However, while dry skin is normal for the pig, excess dandruff is not. Vitamin and/or zinc deficiencies are the most probable causes for this flaky skin and are corrected by improving the diet.

The problem can be covered up by applying glycerine mixed with water or other magic potions to the skin, but it is far better to correct the problem at its source. Oiling your pig is a "cop out" since it ignores the poor diet that is probably causing the problem.

Spaying and Castration

Male pigs that are to be sold as pets are usually castrated at two weeks of age. This procedure is done before the piglet goes to its new home and the new owner is spared the risk and worry of surgery.

If you did purchase a boar and no longer want to put up with the smells and behaviors of a boar, it is never to late to castrate him. Your veterinarian will use anesthesia to perform this surgery on an older animal even though it is usually not used on young piglets.

If you purchased a barrow but notice a very pungent, offensive odor about him, he may be a monorchid. If one testicle was retained up in the abdomen when he was originally castrated, the breeder may have erroneously assumed he only had one testicle and just removed the visible one. A boar with both testicles retained is not fertile, but he still acts and smells like a boar. Retained testicles are an undesirable inherited trait. Removing a retained testicle is a more difficult surgical procedure than routine castration, but it turns an unacceptable pet into a very acceptable one. (People who say that boars don't smell probably keep theirs outdoors!)

Historically, female pigs have not been routinely spayed. At the same time, pigs have not routinely been kept as pets. Pigs have a three week estrus cycle and some females can be quite difficult to live with while they are coming into season and while they are in season. They do not bleed when in season, like dogs, but they moan and groan and cry a lot. This could mean that ten days out of every twenty might be less than pleasant. Some pigs may even lose their housebreaking and urinate in front of family members, especially if there are no boars around for them to seek out.

Pigs can be spayed in a surgery similar to that performed on dogs. Both the ovaries and uterus are removed and the pig will no longer have estrus cycles and will no longer be able to reproduce. This surgery ideally should be performed in young gilts before they have built up extra body fat that may complicate surgery. We are currently spaying piglets prior to weaning and feel there is less stress associated with the procedure at this age.

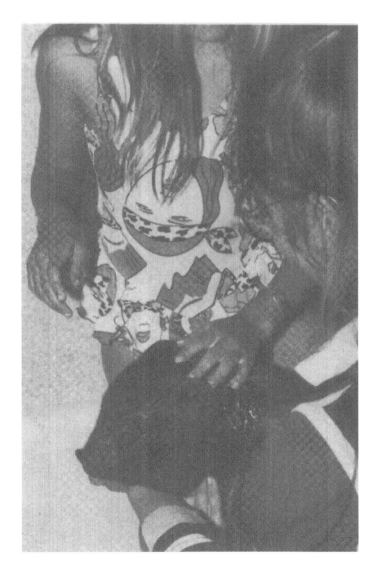

Hog Wash!
Photo by Pattie Washburn

MEDICAL MANAGEMENT

Gastrointestinal System

Pigs can get stomach aches just like we can. If your pig is walking hunched up and can't get comfortable when lying down, he may have an upset stomach. Try to think of what he has eaten recently and whether he has passed urine and stool.

Older babies and adults may also experience different forms of indigestion with the same vague symptoms of discomfort. Some Mylanta, Mylicon, or cultured yogurt may solve the problem quickly. Use the dose on the bottle appropriate for the weight of your pig. If you find yourself treating indigestion more than occasionally, you should approach the problem by working on a more appropriate diet for your pig.

Pigs are also prone to gastric ulcers. These are most commonly associated with improper diet, mental and/or physical stress, infections, or parasitism. They often occur in young piglets during their period of fastest growth, but may occur in any age animal.

Pigs with ulcers periodically go off their feed, become lethargic, grind their teeth in pain, and may have dark, black diarrhea. These pigs are often on a very finely ground and/or corn diet. You should be aware that many of the pelleted diets, both large and small pellets, are prepared from finely ground feeds. Increasing the fiber in the pig's diet goes a long ways in controlling the frequency and severity of ulcer attacks. Try feeding some alfalfa hay each day if your pig is not able to graze in your backyard.

Respiratory System

Pneumonia is a serious problem in farm pigs. The most serious pneumonias are highly contagious from pig to pig. If you keep your pet pig away from other pigs, you can almost completely eliminate the possibility of his becoming infected. Remember that even healthy appearing pigs can be infectious. However, bacteria can be carried in airborne droplets from sneezing and coughing, so direct nose-to-nose contact is not necessary for contagion. Upper respiratory infections involving the nasal passages and possibly the upper airways are more likely to be a problem in pet pigs. The nasal mucus membranes can become irritated and inflamed by many materials that your pig may find to root in. Once inflamed, they are susceptible to overgrowth of bacteria that may already be in residence in the nose or to secondary infection by new bacteria.

A clear, watery nasal discharge is normal for a pig. Any thick, green or yellow discharge from the nose should be considered abnormal. Sneezing or coughing more than two or three times is also not normal. A white or yellow discharge from the eye may also indicate an upper respiratory problem. These signs should not be ignored. You are wisest to treat a pig's minor respiratory problem before it becomes a major one. This is especially true in young, growing piglets who are most prone to Atrophic Rhinitis. Follow your veterinarian's recommendation when choosing the antibiotic to use in treatment.

Do not confuse salivary foam with an abnormal nasal discharge. Most pigs "froth at the mouth" when they are excited about food. This salivary foam builds up around the lips and often drips onto the floor. Boars also develop excess frothy saliva when sexually excited.

Urinary System

Urinary obstruction is a common and difficult problem in ruminants, cats, and occasionally dogs. It is not a reported problem in large breeds of swine.

In fact, veterinary textbooks do not even discuss it. It remains to be seen just how much of a problem this will be in our pet pigs. It is anticipated that the problem might be worse in pet pigs because their diet is not regulated as carefully as the diet of market hogs and also because they live longer than market hogs.

It is suspected that diet imbalances are the primary causes of urinary stones in other animals and are probably equally guilty in similar problems in swine. Maybe if an excellent miniature pig diet is developed and fed exclusive of treats and goodies our pet pigs will fare as well as the market animals. If you are ever concerned that your pig may have urinary problems, encourage water drinking to dilute the urine and flush out the system. Too much water won't hurt your pig and may well avert a serious problem.

Lameness

Pigs can become lame for as many varied reasons as other animals. They are not the most agile of animals and can easily sprain a joint or pull a muscle. This occurs most commonly while they are small and still think they are nimble and when they start jumping off the furniture onto the floor. A couple of days of confinement in a very small area or a crate with secure footing is the ideal first treatment. It prevents reinjury and gives the inflamed or damaged tissue a chance to start healing.

As adolescents, a pig's joints are susceptible to several damaging diseases. Osteochondritis dessicans causes joint injury in the shoulders, elbows, and hips. The lameness from this disease can last 12- 18 months and may cause some permanent problems. Aspirin may be helpful in relieving the worst of the pain. A 325 mg (5 grains) tablet can be given twice daily to an adult pig.

Nutritional arthritis can readily occur in pigs fed improper diets. Improving the diet helps, but does not cure the condition. Aspirin may also be helpful in relieving the worst of the pain in this type of arthritis. Use the same dose as listed for Osteochondritis.

Diet also affects lameness problems if your pig is obese. A pig's bones, joints, and muscles are meant to carry just so much weight. An obese pig is stressing its body with every move it makes. An obese pig is also even less agile than normal and is more likely to trip, fall, or otherwise injure itself. If it also has other lameness problems, the obesity adds insult to injury. Do NOT overfeed your pig!

Geriatrics

Pot-Bellied pigs are a new enough pet that old age is not yet of concern. Until these pigs have been kept as pets for ten or fifteen years, we will not have the data necessary to speak with confidence about the problems of pig geriatrics. We will presume though, that the healthy, well-cared for pet pig will live about twelve to eighteen years.

Obesity is likely to be a major problem in mature and older pigs. Most Pot-Bellied pigs would love to live up to their names and have the fattest pot belly possible - and this is acceptable! A fat belly does NOT imply a fat pig. Even an emaciated pot- bellied pig may have full jowls and a hanging belly. Excess fat is deposited over the entire body and should be measured over the ribs and back. Obesity is a very real health hazard so it is important not to overfeed your pig.

Arthritis is a concern in all older animals. Aspirin, a common treatment for arthritis in humans also works well in pig, and pigs can tolerate aspirin about as well as humans. A 325 mg (5 grain) aspirin given twice a day to an adult pig relieves some of the discomfort of arthritis. Try to give the aspirin with food to help prevent stomach problems. A fat pig suffers more from arthritis than a slimmer pig. Again, don't overfeed your pig!

Parasites

INTERNAL PARASITES are better known as "worms". Many kinds of worms can infect pigs but most are spread directly from pig to pig. Pigs almost never become infected from other domestic animals.

Symptoms of parasite infections vary according to the specific parasite involved. Ascarids (roundworms) cause coughing and possibly a fever in the early stage of infection. This may be followed with diarrhea and it may be difficult to keep the animal in good body condition. A very severe infestation may cause intestinal obstruction. Lungworms cause a subclinical pneumonia and chronic cough. Most of the other nematodes (roundworms) are either not clinically important or cause an animal to be difficult to maintain in good condition. Coccidia, a single celled organism (a protozoa), may cause diarrhea and poor condition. It rarely causes the bloody diarrhea that is seen in other species. Toxoplasma is another protozoa which may cause fever, cough, weakness, diarrhea, and abortions.

Many Pot-Bellied pigs are free of worms. Have your veterinarian run periodic fetal examinations. As long as there are no parasites, there is no need to give the pig any worm medications. If you own an "only pig," you can be reasonably certain that your pig will continue worm-free. If you have other pigs, or visit with other pigs, keep up your routine fecal exams.

Tramisol, Atgard, and Ivomec are all excellent wormers that can be used on pigs. But don't use them unless you prove to yourself that there is a need.

EXTERNAL PARASITES should not be a major problem in pet Pot-Bellied pigs. Dog and cat fleas may be found on pigs occasionally, but do not infest them. The pig skin is too thick and the fleas aren't happy on them. The "stick-tight" fleas from chickens may infest a pig on the thinner skin around the eyes and ears. Ticks may also attach to a pig, but probably prefer your dog or cat.

If your pig has access to market pigs, he may pick up some lice. Pig lice are the largest of sucking lice on domestic animals. They are up to 1/8-1/4 inch long and are grayish brown in color with black markings. They prefer the thinner folds of skin around the neck and jowl, the base and inside of the ears, inside the legs, and the flanks. These lice are very species specific and do not infest humans or domestic animals other than pigs. Louse powder eliminates the lice quickly. Pigs may also develop two forms of mange, Demodectic and Sarcoptic. Demodectic mange in the pig appears as small nodules that may rupture and exude a thick, creamy paste. It does not cause the severe skin involvement and hair loss that is seen in dogs. Demodex, the organism that causes this type of mange, is a species specific organism and does not infest humans or other domestic animals.

Sarcoptic mange is caused by a mite that does infect humans and other animals. It causes severe itching and the pig may do more damage to itself by scratching than the mite itself does. This form of mange may be difficult to diagnose, but once diagnosed, it is easy to treat.

Trained pigs are more fun

PART THREE

TRAINING AND TEACHING

Treat and a backscratch for coming

PSYCHOLOGY AND SWINECHOLOGY

Why Train?

Pig lessons are important because your pig student does not think he needs you. He is not stubborn or willful, just honest in his own self-interest. He will be friendly and cooperative only if it is both easy and enjoyable to be working with you.

At first your pig will only like to eat and sleep. If you approach his lessons correctly, he will soon be eager to travel with you and show off. He will also be much more enjoyable to live with because you will be able to communicate to him what you want him to do.

Pig: Pet or Pest?

Any pet can be a pest if he always gets his own way. How you respond to your pig when he is less than perfect teaches him how to behave. An inventive, alert owner can be more than a match for an intelligent pig.

Picture the pet pig who jumps up on you when you are eating. There are several ways you can respond and each will have a different effect on the pig and his future feelings about .people.

Situation 1. The pig jumps up. You yell at him and chase him out of the room. He feels terrible. He was jumping up to be friendly and to share your food. He thinks you were unreasonably cruel and unfeeling. Chances are he avoids you in the future or becomes even more assertive. This kind of active response on your part is a bad idea.

Situation 2. The pig jumps up and you let him. You learn to resent your own pig. The pig learns to take advantage of you, as well as your family and friends. He becomes a piglet juvenile delinquent who ends up living in a pen or cage. You have created this criminal. This passive response on your part is still a bad idea.

Situation 3. The pig jumps up. You say "NO"! You startle him and buy time while you fumble in your pocket for some pig food. You take this opportunity to teach him to jump down by offering food and tapping a spot on the floor with your finger. You reward him and tell him how smart he is to move right where you told him. He feels good and gets in the habit of sitting next to you to beg for food instead of trying to help himself. You're not upset; he's not upset, and he has learned a good behavior. This time your response is active and a good idea.

In dealing with your pet pig, you have many different options. Some are better than others and it is best to choose what you are going to do rather than just reacting blindly. Curious, friendly pigs do as well, if not better, with redirection and praise rather than punishment.

Redirection

Redirection is a technique that can be used successfully in a variety of different situations. For instance, if your pig is dumping over the wastepaper basket, you should give him a positive command rather than punish him. Call him to you and tell him how wonderful he is. Reward him for coming. With repetition, he gets in the habit of coming to you when he thinks about doing something that you don't like him to do. Praise him every time he comes to you so he has a way of asking for a reward when he needs one.

Water Bottles

Another tactic for handling persistent misbehavior is with a squirt bottle. The pig jumps up and you squirt him with water from a spray bottle. One quick squirt and your pig is insulted and probably forgets what he was doing. He may not even blame you if you act innocent. You pretend that the water is the direct result of what the pig did. Water bottles, or even whole glasses of water, are excellent when dealing with potentially dangerous situations (e.g., getting in the refrigerator) or bad habits.

Trained Pigs Are More Fun

Some of the most fun things to do with pigs involve going places with them. However, if your pig is untrained and always does just as he pleases, you may get a number of nasty surprises when you suddenly try to take him to a Christmas or Valenswines Day party.

Your friends may have a hard time understanding what a great pet you have if he screams whenever you take him out or put him back in his cage. Even if your pig travels willingly, but is too nervous to do anything but eat, he will not be much fun as a traveling companion.

Remember that the unknown is frightening to everyone and a frightened pig can be very uncooperative. Careful training can help prevent new situations from automatically becoming frightening situations.

The goal is to have a confident pig who enjoy traveling and meeting new people. When you want to take him somewhere, either to show off or just to go to the veterinarian's office, it should not be an insurmountable task. Work with your pig often and learn how to do a variety of things with him so you can travel together comfortably.

A trusting relationship between you and your pig is the foundation of all successful training. You can enhance his development if you keep him with you as much as possible. He will accommodate himself to your lifestyle only if the feels that he is a regular part of your life. Trust develops as a result of quality time spent together.

Training Starts Right Now

Training begins the moment you get your new pig, because he will be learning even if you don't think you are teaching. It is not in anyone's best interests to let him "settle in" by putting him in a room and feeding him out of a bowl for a few days. Begin teaching him to like you immediately. Gently shape your pet's behavior while he is getting to know you. He'll do his best to please you if you make your instructions clear, simple, and consistent from the beginning.

What Not To Teach Your Pig

Things you do not want to teach your piglet are as important to know as the things you to want to teach him. Do not encourage him to do anything that will not be cute when he grows up. If you don''t want your 100 lb. adult pig sitting in your favorite chair with you, don't let your 10 lb. baby sit there.

It is always harder to break bad habits later when both you and your pig are set in your ways. Teach him his manners now. It is an investment in his future.

The pig is clever and his nose is strong. Try not to teach your pig how to open the refrigerator. Don't feed the pig out of the refrigerator. Instead, take the food out, put it on the counter, and feed the pig later. So far this has worked well for us and none of the pigs have learned how to open the refrigerator. Any pig fooling around with the refrigerator door is subject to the squirt bottle treatment without warning or explanation.

After raiding the pantry

Never chase your pig
Cartoon by Michael O. Smith

TEACHING TECHNIQUES

There are a few things you should know about how pigs think before you begin to teach new skills to your porcine pet. (1) Piglets think differently than other domestic animals. (2) A piglet's first instinct is self-preservation. (3) Pigs distrust the use of force. (4) Pigs work for food.

Pigs Think Differently

Piglets think differently than other animals. Even if you have had great success training dogs, horses, or other more common domestic animals, don't count on that type of training being a success with your pet pig.

Pigs are unlike animals that have a pack or herd instinct and a "follow the leader" attitude. A group of pigs has a pecking order but remains a gathering of eccentric individualists that all run different directions when they are frightened.

In contrast to other animals, pigs are hedonistic creatures who care very little about social graces and certainly see no reason why anyone would even want to be in charge (contrary to Orwell's depiction of them in ANIMAL FARM). Pigs are confidently self-contented. They respect each other, but act independently. Sir Winston Churchill is credited with saying "A cat looks down on a person, a dog looks up to you, but a pig looks on yours an equal." It is entirely up to you to become his friend.

Pigs Are Hunted in the Wild

A pig's first instincts are fear and self-preservation. A piglet runs from danger because he has no claws or fangs for defense. In the wild, piglets are in danger of being eaten, so smart piglets run fast.

Your piglet learns by what he does. He learns either fear or confidence as a direct result of how you control his life. A pig is the most intelligent of domestic animals, so he learns quickly. Once he has learned a response to a given action, either good or had, he is very slow to forget.

Do Not Force Pigs

Pigs distrust force. Never force a pig! Your training should use the gentle art of guiding not forcing.

If you chase a pig he probably does not remember how nice you were after you caught him. He remembers running away and being afraid of you. If you never chase, he will never run and you will not reinforce his natural (but unwanted) instinct.

A pig's mind works on an immediate-response basis. Use it to your advantage or it will work against you. It takes two to fight so it is up to you to cal for a cease-fire.

Discipline

Discipline should be very gentle with a pig. During training he disciplines himself by backing away from you and the food. This is punishment enough for any pig. He learns from the anticipation of reward - not from the fear of punishment.

For serious misbehavior, researchers feel that the most effective discipline is crowding the pig into a wall. You should push at his neck near the corner of his jaw and immobilize him for a few seconds. This maneuver closely duplicates how pigs fight, where the loser is lifted off his front feet by the winner who gets under his throat.. A modified version of this is to take the pig's head in your hands and talk seriously to him for a few seconds.

Training vs. Instinct

The basis of most training is teaching animals to do things that are close to what they would do in the wild. We reinforce their instincts. However, this is not the case with pet pigs. Many of the behaviors you may wish to teach your pig are not only behaviors they would not do in the wild, but are the very behaviors that would leave them most vulnerable to predators.

A predator reaches down over the top of the piglet, grabs the piglet by the shoulder or chest, squeezes the piglet, and carries him off to eat. A loving owner wants to reach down over the top of the piglet, grab under or around its chest, pick it up and give it a big hug. The piglet's instincts cannot differentiate between predator and loving owner. With the proper training, you will be able to catch, pick-up, hug, and carry your piglet. He will even enjoy it, even though his instincts associate all of these things with certain death.

Reward

"Honest work for honest wages." It is important to reward your pig in a way that he feels is intrinsically valuable. "The way to a pig's heart is though his stomach" should become your motto when dealing with these little pigs. You get the best results if you are associated with his food.

Do not make a habit of feeding him without asking him to do something for his food reward, and never ask him to do something without rewarding him for his best effort. NO FREE LUNCHES. Use his pig food rations for obtaining results. Once he knows you are the keeper of the piggy kibble you will have his attention.

Basic-training

Program your pig for success by feeding him when he TRIES to do what you want. This is not bribery, but simple honest wages. Take things one step at a time. You might just ask him to come and sit for his breakfast. Food given with a pat and a "good pig" teaches him to love you and not his food dish.

Try to end every training session on a winning note. This is important. He has worked hard trying to understand you, and he needs the reassurance of your praise, reward, and approval.

Remember, a pig thinks of the enjoyment of the moment. He is only interested in what is happening right this minute. He is not interested in tomorrow, and he is not very interested in yesterday or even a minute ago. He is also extremely forgiving if he was not badly frightened.

Bonding

Training allows a bond to form between you and your pig. It provides mental stimulation and human interaction which is good for the pig, even if he learns nothing of great importance. The offer of a treat is the only way he can be certain of what you expect of him. This understanding produces the bonding which is the way to have a pet pig you can be proud of and enjoy for many years.

Spend time with your pig doing almost nothing. After he has trained and eaten, sit with him. If he is still hesitant he may at least sneak up to you to investigate and sniff. If he is tamer he will enjoy being petted and scratched. If there is no more food around and he still hangs out with you, you know the bond is forming.

Timing and the Art of Training

Your goal should be to ask just a little more of your pig each day. Start with something easy first. Break each new lesson into several smaller rewarding opportunities. Go back to something easy when he fails, then work up to harder requests a step at a time. If a lesson becomes a problem, take smaller steps or try a different way of teaching the same thing. Be generous when he succeeds. Finish with something easy enough that he is able to do it and reward him well for being so smart.

Application of these principles allows you to calm the pig so he uses his brain and not his fear reflexes. You will be able to gain control of the pig so that he enjoys doing what you want.

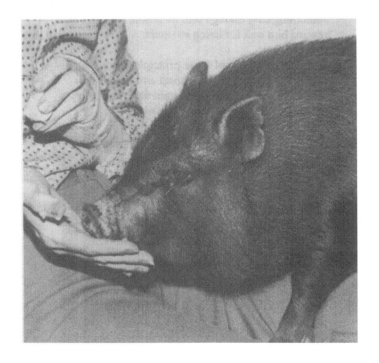

Eating out of the palm of your hand

PIG HANDLING

With love and gentleness, allow your piglet to learn to volunteer himself into your control. He needs to know that he can move toward you and away from you without danger. He needs to learn to eat out of your hand and to let you touch him. A cooperative pet pig must learn a series of different skills.

Never chase your pig; predators chase pigs. He will only learn to run from you. It is unnatural for a pig to let himself be caught so you want to make it especially easy for him. You want your pig to think of you as a good friend, not as a predator.

Lesson Preparation

Think ahead so you can avoid problems. You pick the time and the place for training. Don't let yourself be rushed, as it clouds your judgment and steals your patience. Your piglet is very intelligent and if you don't plan things out, you could just as easily become the trainee rather than the trainer.

Walking Confidently Ahead of You

A pet pig is normally trained to walk just in front of his owner - not beside or behind him (al- though some people and pigs prefer walking beside or be- hind). Teaching your pig to walk in front of you without being frightened is an important step. At first he will keep as far away from you as possible, but as he learns to trust you he will let you come closer and closer before he moves. Herd him slowly, step by step, as slowly as possible, by staying at a distance.

The goal is to move your piglet at a steady walk directly in front of you. He will usually try to trot away, but you should concentrate on making him stay close and not run away from you. Do this by moving him inch by inch, so as not to excite him Pigs and people think more clearly when they are not upset.

Catching Your Pig

When trying to catch your pig, keep moving him into a progressively smaller area. When he is in an area the size of a small bathroom or closet, slowly, step by step, inch by inch, move closer. If he jumps past you, catch him in mid-air or let him go and start over more slowly. Sometimes you can back him into a corner and then inch your hand under his chin and catch even a fairly nervous pig gently.

Once you are close to the pig, offer him food!!!!!! As he eats out of your hand, pick him up or push him around with your free hand. Even a very large pig benefits from learning to let you maneuver him from side to side, and forward and back. Make certain he enjoys the experience. Spend some time sitting quietly, loving him, and feeding him. Don't rush things too fast. Allowing you to control his body is an important skill for your pig to learn. This simple skill is the basis for much of his future training.

Eating Out of the Palm of your Hand

You gain more control over your pig by feeding him tidbits than with any leash or cage. You can use food to get, keep, and hold his attention.

At first, each time you touch him you may scare him and cause him to run away, leaving the food behind him. If you do not reinforce this fear by forcing or chasing him, it quickly disappears . He is very curious and very fond of food.

Each time he is touched or held while he is eating he is learning to like being touched and held. He is learning to trust you to do things he likes. Pig logic works like this:

> Food = good,
> (I get food when I get touched)
> touched = food,
> (so touched must be ok)
> touched = good.

Biting the Hand That Feeds

Pot-Bellied pigs, unlike some other breeds, rarely bite unless mistreated. Many bottle babies however have a hard time learning they can not bite fingers because fingers feel like baby bottle nipples.

All animals, especially babies, need to learn the difference between fingers and food. Try not to let your piglet chew on your fingers and if he nibbles on them say "OUCH"!

Pigs are smart and are always trying to figure things out. At first your piglet may seem to think if he finds the right place to bite, the hand automatically dispenses food. He soon learns that you only squeal and take your hand away.

One pig I raised would grab my hand and move it in front of my face as if to say "look this is empty, where is the food?" She was gentle, but it was startling at first until I understood why she wanted to carry my hand in her mouth. It is important for owners to try to figure out what their gigs are saying.

When you think your piglet almost has the idea, you may add another lesson. Teach him to lick food like peanut butter or cream cheese off your fingers without hurting you. At the first touch of a tooth, jerk your hand away and play act at being afraid for a few seconds.

Finally, teach him to let you hold food in your fist without letting him have it. He can push and nuzzle, but at the first gentle bite, the hand is pulled out of the way. Reward him after he has been patient by giving him a treat.

Never risk these lessons with more than one animal at a time. Pigs competing for food are very focused on the food. They get in a feeding frenzy and they can't learn.

Don't be boorish about these lessons. Remember that lessons can be frustrating; but not eating fingers is definitely a skill your pig needs to learn.

Learning to "Sit"

An excellent skill to practice is sitting. Your pig will hesitate at first because he would rather remain on his feet ready to run, but you can gain his confidence. Pigs sit because they have a hard time looking up at you for their food from a standing position. Hold the food just out of reach above his nose. As he starts to move his head up and back, move the food back so it stays just out of reach.

As always, start by rewarding for any partial progress. Reward him for putting his head up, then for starting to bend his rear legs. When he actually sits all the way down, praise and reward him again.

Learning "Down"

Down is a complete change of gears for a pig. Once the pig is finished eating, scratch his back and as he relaxes he will lay down. First, start scratching his rump and he will sit; then scratch his shoulders or armpit and he will lay all the way down. Soon, if you touch him on any of his favorite spots he will drop down and roll on his side for a tummy rub. A pig needs to feel safe before he will lie down.. This is one trick some pigs never learn.

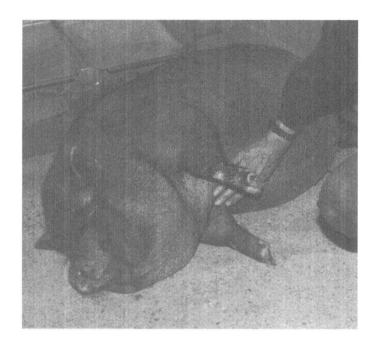

Tummy Rub

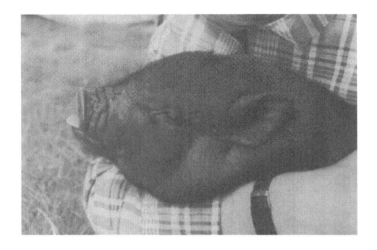

Nestled in the crook of your elbow

CATCHING AND HOLDING

Catching your pig can become easier each time you do it or it can become a greased pig contest. Practice catching your pig. Patience and reward at this basic stage of training encourages your pig to trust you. This trust carries over into all your future training. Ignore the temptation to chase and grab your pig and then make friends afterwards. You may catch him faster at first, but he will lose ground on his overall training. The following suggestions are the result of much trial and error. Learn from our mistakes. Try it, you'll like it.

Lap Training

If your pig is small enough, start with lap training. Sit on the floor, offer food and wait for your piglet to climb into your lap for more food..He learns to climb into your lap one small step at a time. He deserves a reward for trying to come closer than he did a moment before, which is probably closer than he feels is safe. Give and take while he learns that if he moves to you he gets a piece of food, but if he moves away he can not reach the food. Be flexible, each time he retreats, you may have to reach farther out to feed him again. On each approach, he should come faster and closer to you before he retreats a in. When he is very close, fill his mouth with food. Slip your other hand behind him and boost him into your lap. This is the easiest technique for catching your pig without resorting to chasing or forcing.

Pen Training

Using a pen is another way you can train your pig to let you catch and hold him. Start with a very narrow pen. Think ahead and pick your time and place so that you have all of the advantages. Go very slowly, offer him food, and try not to get him too upset to eat. Use the food to lead him as much as possible. Herd him into a corner or into a smaller area of the pen. By moving slowly and patiently, step by step, inch by inch, he has time to get used to the idea without getting excited or feeling forced. Make certain that he finds it a rewarding experience so he wants to do it again next time. Once you get, him where you want him, sit quietly, pet him, and feed him whatever he likes. You can use his regular food or a special treat. As he calms down, corner him slowly and pick him up or push him into your lap (or wherever it is you want him).

Pig Panel Training

If you have a large or frightened pig, corner him slowly in an area with solid walls. Use a pig panel, so he does not have to learn to deal with people just yet. A pig panel is a solid piece of ply- wood with hand holds, that is taller than the pig's head and about the same length as the pig. How it is made is not important. It lets you move the pig in an impersonal way, so he does not have to look at you. Use it to slowly move him into a corner. Once confined in the corner, reach over the pig panel and pet and feed him as he calms down. You can gradually convince him that this is a pleasant experience.

Above all, be patient. He may have good reason to be afraid of people. You are teaching him something that goes against everything he has known and everything that centuries of instinct tell him. Remember that pigs are often more cooperative when they are not rushed.

Choose Your Method

Always adjust your behavior to what your pig can cope with at the time. Moments saved now with a hasty catch will cost you hours before he learns to trust you completely. We speak from experience. We have tried the hasty catch methods and the patient catch methods. The results have been far superior in the long run when we took more time in the beginning.

How To Hold Your Piglet

Your piglet likes to be held piglet fashion with his head and body at the same level. Support his throat and rear end. Do not hold him by his stomach. That is uncomfortable because it puts too much pressure on his belly. Your piglet may complain often, and loudly, that he is uncomfortable while you are learning to hold him. Cradle him in your arms with both his nose and rear end safe in the crooks of your elbows. Being held "level" feels safer to a pig because he feels more like he is lying on the floor. Let his feet dangle - it is safer for you if he wiggles because you can position those sharp hooves away from you.

This is very different from the way a puppy or kitten likes to be held, but a mother pig never carries her babies, so you are working with a different set of reflexes.

While Holding Your Pig

Feed your pig as often as possible while you are holding or stroking him. Eating while in your arms teaches him to prefer being held. You want your pig to prefer your company and to enjoy being handled. If he doesn't like being held, feed him all his meals while he is in your arms. He'll quickly learn to like being in your arms.

Hold and carry your pig as much as you comfortably can. Do it now, he will not get any smaller! But remember that when he is older, he will still never be too large to hold in your arms while he is standing on the ground.

Restraint

Your pig should learn that it is safe to let you restrain him. Control is most efficiently maintained with one hand under his chin ready to lift up gently while he is backed into a corner or against your other hand. Holding him now can make him more tractable as he grows. Don't forget to reward him with food during the lesson.

Knowing when to give up is important also. If your pig screams or is very restless, chances are he needs a break. When ear rubs and reassurance don't work, put your pig down or in his crate for a few moments. This is not the time to hang on to him whether he likes it or not. If you force him he learns how to fight you, and with practice he will fight harder and harder next time.

Hogs and Kisses

Pigs don't hug and kiss each other. If your pig complains when you hug or kiss him, don't feel rejected. Understand that like so many other things, you need to teach him to like this strange new thing humans do. When you smack your lips to kiss him it says something rude in pig language. Reward him for taking it gracefully, and soon he will enjoy your attentions.

Making friends at the pigs level

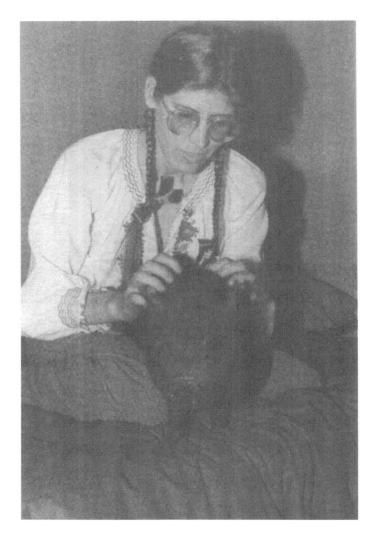

Spend time getting to know your piglet

COMING AND FOLLOWING

Getting Your Pig's Attention

Pigs are so curious that if you sit still they usually come to investigate. If they get food, then they think you are worth investigating.

Sit or lay on the floor so you don't tower over your pig. Sound like you are eating something wonderful. Smack your hips or eat something noisy like a juicy apple. Sit still, and talk softly. A tidbit or a treat is the curious pig's pay-off. Practice until, when you sit down, he automatically comes over to you.

Teaching "Come"

After your pig has learned to come to you for food, he is ready for the next step, coming when you whistle or call. Start by whistling or calling when he is already coming. Always make it worth his while to come to you, and soon he will come running any chance he gets. If he gets one piece of food for coming over to you any time and several pieces of food for coming when called, he will soon learn to come to you, and soon he will come running any "come" on command.

One common mistake is teaching your pig to come when you rattle food in a can or dish. Avoid doing this because it requires props you may not always have with you. You can just as easily teach your pig to come when you call or whistle.

Follow Me

When your pig expects to get food for coming to you, introduce a new game. Call your pig as you walk away and your pig will learn to follow.

At first reward his following by feeding him every few steps. Then, as he progresses, feed him less often. Remember the goal is not a contest to see how rarely you have to feed him. Try to feed him often to keep his attention on you. If you feed too much at one time he will stop while he concentrates on eating, so use small treats. A single piece of pig food or equivalent size treat is more than adequate.

Going For A Walk

Once your pig has learned to follow, start going places. As always, start easy, then get more complicated. Start by going back and forth in his territory: the backyard, his pen, or in the house. Be inventive as you practice. Try going in and out, up and down, over and even under obstacles in your yard.

Teaching Climb Up

If you tap on the floor with a piece of food your pig should automatically move right there to investigate and get the food, Build on this tendency until you use it to get him into, onto, and out of different places. My pigs learn to follow my tapping and go almost anywhere I want them. This same skill gets them out of places where they are unwanted.

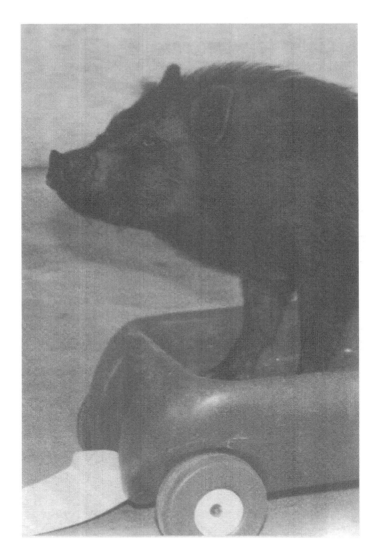

Learning to step up

CRATE TRAINING

Crates are not cruel; they can actually be a "magic carpet" for your pet. They give your pig more freedom because he can go places he couldn't go without one. However, never use the crate as punishment! This is a sure way to undo all the positive aspects of crate training.

Pigs that have already traveled in a crate may be especially fond of sleeping in their crate and this is a good skill to keep ready for future use.

Why Crate Training

It is essential for your pig to learn to spend some time in his crate because if crates are familiar friendly places to your pig he will always be ready for the unexpected. Travel is greatly facilitated because your pig has a home base. A crate trained pig is prepared if you need to ship him on an airplane or if he ever needs to stay at a boarding kennel or the veterinarians. People who are skeptical of pigs will feel more comfortable letting you visit if you tell them he can stay in his crate. A well behaved pig who happily goes into and out of his crate does a lot to convince people that pigs are as nice as dogs.

Basics of Crate Training

Get a nice big crate so your pig can turn around easily. This will be a very large crate for adult pigs because they are long-bodied. Prepare the crate by putting in a non-skid floor covering and either prop the door open or take it off.

The first lessons are getting into the crate on his own, then getting into the crate for you on command.

How To Crate Train

Start training by tossing small amounts of food into the back of the crate. All pigs have an excellent sense of smell and soon figure out that there is food in the crate. Some pigs feel safer going in alone at first. If you send them in for food often, they soon relax and let you watch, then let you actually send them in. When your pig is bold and confident about entering the crate he is ready to learn more. Put a handful of food into the crate when he is hungry and while he gobbles it up quietly lock the door behind him. Reassure him at first by giving him a treat and letting him out again almost immediately. Start leaving him alone in his crate for longer and longer times. Don't punish him by locking him up when he can hear your or see you doing other things. He will feel left out. An ideal time to train is at your bed-time.

Shipping Crate

When I send piglets on airplanes I usually fill the crate about half full of hay. The piglets are first introduced to crates in my back room. They go to the crate whenever they want a snack. They soon associate the crate with a nice meal. This method of crate training minimizes the stress of shipping (and keeps hay from being spread all over my house!).

Hay is a multi-purpose substance. When used in a shipping crate, the pig can eat it, play with it, or relax, chewing it like gum. He often covers the door with it to block out the sounds, or he may burrow under it to feel safer. It is also absorbent if he has an accident.

Once in his new home, the crate can be a security blanket. It is something familiar in a strange new world.

Using Crate Training

We have already mentioned traveling in the crate, and staying in strange or inhospitable places in the crate. The crate can also be an excellent housebreaking aid because the pig does not mess in his crate unless he is frightened, or left in it a long time.

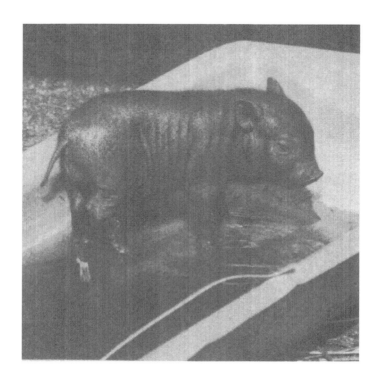

Mini Swine Cooler

Crate Training

HOUSE BREAKING

First Lessons

Make it easy for the piglet. Start housebreaking the minute you get home. First, take your pig outside, then give him a drink and let him explore for a few minutes. If after a few minutes he has still not urinated, take him back inside. Then keep him with you every minute. When you have to put him down, take him outside or put him in a crate. He doesn't know his way around yet, but he will not mess in his bed if he can help it. If he does mess in his crate clean it out and put him back in. In a few hours he will need to go again. Take him outside and try again.

Housebreaking actually starts when the piglet is born, so a properly raised piglet has a head start. A piglet should grow up in an environment where he can go in or out as he needs to. Piglets usually start going to the far end of their area by the time they are are 2-3 weeks old to urinate and defecate. They still have to urinate frequently at eight weeks, but they are fairly safe in the house and car. By twelve weeks they are safe for several hours, and by sixteen weeks they can wait all day by themselves if necessary.

Housebreaking Specifics

A piglet usually urinates each time he wakes up and when he exercises. You can make his house- breaking easier if you take him out at these times. Always take your piglet out first thing in the morning, when you get home from work, and just before bedtime.

If you are holding him and you notice that he is getting restless, take him out and put him down on the ground. Pigs usually don't scratch or circle when they need to go out. They do get a preoccupied expression, but it is hard to recognize. Take your piglet out often but only for a few minutes at a time.

One thing that is hard to understand is that if your pig has been out for several hours and you bring him inside, he still probably needs to go out again soon. Pigs usually urinate shortly after they first go out the door and then they forget to go again because they get busy exploring.

Environment

Build a temporary, small pen outside a back door. A roll of welded wire cage material works well for this. Check the sides and bottom of the pen carefully. Remember, that an unattended pig naturally roots and may find a way out underneath.

Make sure this pen is a nice quiet, private place to urinate. If dogs and children are bouncing all over the pen, your piglet may feel that the secluded spot under the dining room table is much more appropriate.

Rectangular pens are the best for teaching. If he spends much time there, put his bed at one end and his food and water in the middle. He will almost always mess in the far end, away from his bed and food.

Litter Box Training

If you are away from home for long periods during the day, you may decide that a litter box is the best way for your family to handle housebreaking.

Put the litter box at the far end of his pen or room. Choose a box that is not too tall, but easy to get into. Fill it half full with nontoxic white pine wood shavings. Use shavings instead of kitty litter because shavings do not cause problems if the piglet eats them.

Make sure he has a nice bed at the other end of the room, because if the litter box is the softest warm bed he will sleep in it. Pigs are practical.

Houses with stairs may need two litter boxes as it is a gymnastic feat for a ten pound piglet to climb a flight of stairs with a full bladder.

Dog Doors

A dog door is fine to start teaching house breaking, but it does not teach your pig to wait to go out. Consider dog doors as a half way stage of housebreaking, or you will have piggy accidents when you visit away from home.

Teach your pig to go in and out the dog door just as you teach every other new skill, one step at a time. Start by teaching him to go out with the flap held up. Tempt him to go though with food and reward him when he does. Then teach him to come in, and finally teach him to go through the flap by himself. Incidentally most pigs need a large size door, set fairly low near the floor. You can housebreak your pig at the same time you teach him to use the door by taking him out frequently using the dog door.

Crate Assisted Training

A pig prefers not to eliminate if he is confined m a small space. His crate can be this place if you let him out frequently. Confine him long enough so that he needs to go, but not so long that he is forced to mess in the crate.

Use crate training as a way to prevent accidents, when you start teaching him to wait to go out. By keeping him somewhere he is reluctant to urinate you are making it easier for him to wait for an opportunity to go someplace more suitable.

Take him out frequently to the place you have prepared for him to urinate and defecate. If he does not urinate in a minute or two, take him right back to his crate. By not leaving him outside to play or sleep all the time he learns faster. After going in and out a few times, let your pig loose in the house but continue to take him outside on the same schedule. He must be able to count on you to let him out as soon as possible when you wake up in the morning, when you come home in the afternoon, and late at night. Remember that success is partly training and partly the physical maturity that allows him to wait so long.

Confinement

Keeping your pig in only one part of the house may make housebreaking harder. A room that is not in his usual territory may be a handy latrine. Since he prefers an out of the way private place to eliminate, when you introduce new rooms, repeat the housetraining. Allow him into the new area but take him back to his usual area to eliminate, before he has an accident.

Asking To Go Out

A pig can learn to ask to go out if you take him out when he squeals. He can also learn to ring a bell.

Problems

Sudden changes in elimination patterns may indicate medical problems. If a pig seems to be straining or trying to urinate too often he may have a urinary tract problem or an upset stomach.

Water

Piglets often urinate when they drink. Offer water outside. Adults do best with two water dishes, and often drink from one and urinate in the other. This is normal and they are trying to keep their area clean.

Accidents

If you catch your piglet having an accident, distract him and take him out immediately. Wait for him to calm down; he may finish urinating outside. Usually he forgets what he was doing and won't go, but try anyway.

More often you will just find a puddle. If your pig has an accident, go back to keeping him with you or keeping him confined for a few hours then taking him out for a minute or two. Repeat the procedure until he eliminates outside routinely. Praise him each time and continue to concentrate on preventing accidents. Never punish your pig.

Females

Girl pigs have more trouble learning to be house clean than neutered males or spayed females. When they have their breeding cycles they often have about two accidental puddles a month.

Bad Weather

The more inclement the weather, the more important it is to reward your pig for going outside. It can be hard for him to understand why he should go out in the rain, snow, or other bad weather. It does not make sense to him unless you come outside with him and there is a reward.

Rewards

Feed him a bit when he goes out in the cold or dark to eliminate, because it would have been easier and more practical, he thinks, to mess in the house. You can teach your pig to urinate on command by saying something special and feeding him when he eliminates. Soon, whenever you say that something special, he will go.

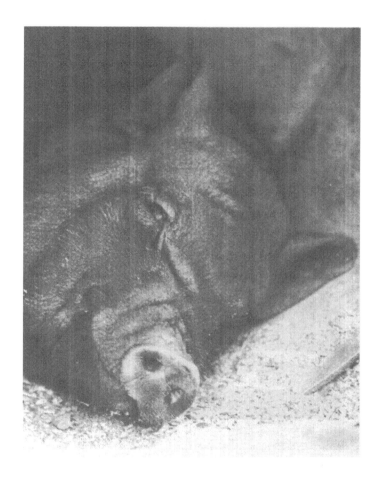

Contented Sow

Learning about car rides

CAR RIDES

Riding happily and safely in a car is an important skill for your pet pig to learn. Being able to easily take your pig with you in the car, wherever and whenever you want to, makes your pet a much more enjoyable companion.

How To Ride In Cars

Sometimes it is easier to teach things in reverse. Teaching your pig about car rides can come before you teach your pig to get into the car by himself. After carrying the pig into the car, feed him a special treat, then go for a short ride. Stop frequently to talk to, feed, and pet your pig.

Pleasant first car rides convince your pig to associate the car ride with good food. Drive smoothly and try to avoid traffic jams which may lead to car sickness. Make him feel safe by bringing a favorite pillow or blanket from home. Do not let him near the driver's seat where he could get into trouble. If your pig needs more encouragement to enjoy car rides, feed him even less in the house and more in the car.

Be careful to avoid excess heat while your pig is riding in the car. It is easier for a pig to overheat than a dog. A pig neither sweats nor pants. He cannot keep himself cool. Being even slightly warm causes him to be restless. To encourage him to ride quietly so he doesn't wander under the driver's feet, turn up the air conditioning.

If he overheats, he may loose his housebreaking. He will also remember not liking the car ride and be less cooperative next time.

How To Get Into The Car

Remember how important it is not to force your pig, but to work with him. If your pig climbs onto your lap, up stairs, onto your bed or sofa, he is ready to learn to get into the car by himself. If the car is a truck or van, which is a big step up, a ramp mounting platform can speed things up, but he can learn to get in.

Caution! Do not try to load your pig into a car if you are parked where it would be dangerous for him to get loose. With the car parked someplace safe, like a fenced yard, walk your pig to the car and tap on the edge of the floor with food just out of his reach. Tell him "UP" as if he was getting into your lap, or onto something he is already used to. If he has practiced putting his front feet up on things he will now learn to put his front feet up on the floor of the car.

If he is accustomed to you pushing his rump into place, then he should continue eating while you position him, so he can get into the car easily. Put some food in front of him, just out of his reach, and give him a push from behind to help him get all the way in. Make sure he gets that food just as he gets in, before he can panic and try to get out. If he gets out without eating your progress will be much slower.

Next, wait until he is hungry, then when he asks for food, have him follow you out to the car. Get into the driver's seat, but leave the passenger door open and call the pig to come to you. As always offer food and feed tiny bits each step of the way, but withhold food when he backs up. Keep encouraging him as long as he is working at the problem. Feed him a whole handful when he succeeds and praise him.

If he gives up and goes off to eat the flowers, take him back inside immediately without feeding him. Remember, for each lesson he gets food only for trying to do what you like, not for going back to the house. Don't give up if your pig is slow to learn to get into the car. Give him time and encouragement. The extra fun you have together will more than make up for the extra work.

Waiting In The Car

Leaving a pig in the car can be as dangerous as leaving a small child there. It can get too hot or too cold, especially if the windows are closed. Pigs are especially vulnerable to heat stroke. The only safe way to leave a pig in a car is to stay with him at all times. If that means a cold cramped night for you, then you will understand that it was cold for your pig also.

Going for a walk
Photo by Pattie Washburn

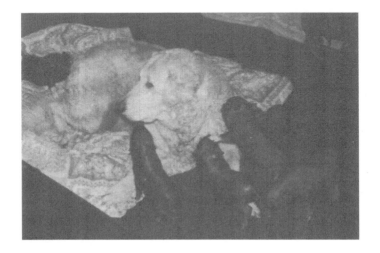

Root Hog and Dog
Photo Courtesy Dr. Blackburn

HARNESSES

Custom Harness

Cat harnesses work for small piglets. A dog harness with an adjustable neck and chest may work for growing pigs. Often you will want to make a custom pig harness.

A velcro figure 8 or "H" pattern harness can work for all ages. Our custom harnesses are made from bright colored nylon webbing with 12 inches of extra strong velcro. They stay put, and can be fastened quickly on a wiggling pig or piglet. Use his out-grown cat harness as a pattern to create or make a new one.

Putting On A Harness

Putting the harness on your pig can be facilitated by getting him to sit in your lap or backing him into a corner with you in front of him. Your pig should be fed almost continuously while you put an his harness. Remember, at each step your pig should be allowed to run away, if he is willing to do without food.

Put your hand through the neck of the harness and as your pig eats food from your hand slip the harness over one ear and then the other. Adjust the harness snugly. Once the harness is on the pig and he has had a short cooling off period, readjust the harness until it stays on and you can still slip one or two fingers under the straps.

Avoid leaving the harness on for long periods as it can make your pig sore. A sore pig won't like you, or the harness, very much.

Walking On A Leash

Walking on a leash is very threatening to a pig at first. The leash pulls on the harness, pinching his shoulders where a predator would bite him. It is very hard for you, as a person with a leash in your hand, to resist the urge to pull on that leash to force him to do what you want.

When first training, avoid pulling on the leash for two reasons. The pig hates it and stops cooperating when you pull. In addition, the harness may slip right off over his shoulders.

You can teach your pig to let you pull on the leash by feeding him as you pull gently. At first if you pull too hard your pig will over react with a terrified tantrum, he may fly into the air screaming and flip over. The only way to stop this is to let go of the leash. Then you can start over. Gradually your pig will learn to accept the guidance of a leash.

Once he walks well on a leash and harness, teach him to walk with just a leash looped around his neck. This way is very useful because then you can improvise a leash at any time from a belt or shoe lace.

Graduate slowly to going for walks to many unfamiliar places. Teach him to go confidently.

Pig and Pups
Photo by Heather Kingdon

GLOSSARY

Language holds many keys to the history of things.
One of the interesting things about pigs is he
richness of the special jargon used to talk about them.
It seems to me clear evidence of the high
regard man has had for pigs, that there are more terms
for talking about pigs than for any other animal that I
know of. It also pleases me that young maiden piglets
are called gilts, a word that also means covered with
gold.

When shopping for your pet pig, don't buy a "pig in a
poke." The following definitions relate to
the sex, age, etc. of pigs and are commonly used
terminology.

BARROW - a neutered male
BOAR - an unaltered male
FARROW - to give birth to piglets
FEEDERS - pigs past the delicate just weaned stage
GILT - a young female
HOG - 120 lb. to 190 lb. or larger
PIG - swine under 120 lb.
PIGLET - baby pig
RUNT - undersized pig, often unhealthy (but if it
lives it often grows as large as its brothers)
SOW - a mature female

STAG - a male neutered after sexual maturity (8-12 weeks of age in Pot-Bellied pigs); usually done to control the strong odor
SWINE - a generic term for all ages, but usually referring to large animals
WEANER - recently weaned from mother's milk

ABOUT THE ILLUSTRATIONS

Photographs: If not otherwise credited are by Kayla or Marden Mull.

Cartoons: Michael O. Smith including cover illustrations.

iii   Walker, age three months, enjoying the wrong end of an ice cream cone.

iv Pigms on her first birthday, filming for PBS television (P for Public not Pork). Jamie Washburn, age 9, leading her. Photo by Lee Wood of Pattie and Lee Photography.

xi Gretel Appleyard is the eight week old "covergirl" piglet in this photo called "Hoglet Kisses". Photo by George A. Reynolds, L.A. Daily News.

xii Elizabeth Ann's babies waiting for dinner. Photo by Heather Kingdon.

xv It is hard tell who is more amazed at seeing the other, the piglet or the crowd. Hamlet, age four and one-half months, in Beverly Hills for Valenswine's Day.

xvi Piggy Sue, age four months on the Blackburn family Christmas card. The only way she will ever be seen with an apple in her mouth. Photo by Dr. Michael Boldrick.

PART ONE

2 Cuddles, eight weeks old, meets grandchild, Lonnie Yokum, with grandfather, Richard Reinbold. Photo by George A. Reynolds, L.A. Daily News.

11 Pig May Leon, at five days old, held level so she feels safe and well supported. She is too young to leave her mother for more than a few minutes, but she is learning to trust humans from the start.

12 Cast Iron, a two year old boar, is strong and athletic. He shows good form as he enjoys running "full boar" back to his pen.

26 Oliver, age two and one-half ninths, takes a ninth inning stretch after arriving in an airline shipping crate.

36 Hamlet, six months, and Dr. Dolittle's Gub Gub, ten months, outgrowing the baby-bath tub.

43 Pig Tails, shown here at three days, being fed pig milk replacer by Dr. Blackburn. Photo by Allie Blackburn.

PART TWO

44 Franklin the Pot-Bellied Pet Pig, age three
months, ready to run or to be caught.

46 Hamlet, age three months, and magician Chris
Blackmore. Photo courtesy of Chris Blackmore,
magician.

52 Elizabeth Ann avoids swimming if she can. Photo
by Heather Kingdon.

59 Piglet, two weeks old, yawning in front of her
heated brooder box. Sire: Cast Iron, Dam: Mumbly
Pig.

60 Cast Iron, age one year, in good weight and show-
ing the tusks, thick hard skin, and froth-
ing at the mouth which are characteristics a boars.

68 This piglet being educed to having a bath. One
person feeds the piglet and the other
washes the piglet.

78 Tough Guy, age nine months, on Rodeo Drive,
Beverly Hills. Ensemble by Garyk Lee.

PART THREE

80 Mumbly Pig, age three years, pregnant and fat. A
gentle sow who is naturally tame.

87 Hamlet, age six months, after a pig out. He has powdered milk all over his face. Notice this picture also shows his nicely trimmed hooves.

95 Tammy Fay Bacon, age five months, learns to climb into my lap for food. She is too large to carry but not too large to hold.

103 Agnes, age two years, obese, before careful dieting.

104 Pigms, at four months, rests comfortably in the crook of my arm while she sticks her tongue out.

111 Pignatious, age six months. Piglets are more curious about things and people who are a level where they can see better. Photo by Lee Arnone.

112 Spending time getting to know Pignatious. Photo by Lee Arnone, actress, and photographer.

116 Piglets are furry at 6 months, this one demonstrates getting up on things for a treat. This skill is useful for teaching lots of things like getting into the car.

121 Piglet, two weeks old, takes his first bath a mini-swine lake made from a snow sled. Sire: Cast Iron, Dam: Fuzzy Wuzzy.

122 Hamlet, age three months, with Blackmore and Gold. Photo courtesy of Chris Blackmore who finds

new things to teach with crate training. Hamlet's job is to disappear.

131 A gilt, guilt free, asleep in a barrel In the shade.

132 An older piglet waits in the car while Kayla holds a piglet and shows him that "cars are nice places." Photo by Pattie Washburn.

137 Pigms, age three months and very overweight, being led by Jamie Washburn age eight. Early leash walking should be done on a loose leash go where the piglet wants to go without pulling. Photo by Pattie Washburn.

138 Piggy Sue's piglets, age two weeks, playing with Sophie, a Golden Retriever. Photo by Lorrie Blackburn, D.V.M.

142 Elizabeth Ann and Border Collie puppies. Photo by Heather Kingdon.

152- The End

POT-BELLIED PIGS

ABOUT THE AUTHORS

KAYLA MULL is a Microbiologist. Her "Creatures of Comfort Miniature Pet Pigs" have been featured in national publications including: Life Magazine, Entrepreneur, Weekly Reader, Seventeen Magazine and People Magazine. She and her pigs have appeared on radio, TV shows and News casts around the world, including: Regis & Kathie Lee, A.M. Los Angeles, The BBC News, Eye on Australia and Inside Edition. Kayla initially majored in Animal Science, and has been employed by zoo's, museums of natural science, and veterinary hospitals. Kayla is a licensed Animal Health Technician and a Clinical Laboratory Technologist.

LORRIE BLACKBURN, D.V.M.(aka Lorrie Boldrick, D.V.M.) is a graduate of U.C. Davis, and a member of the American Association of Swine Practitioners. Her small animal veterinary practice includes goats, sheep, miniature pigs, and exotic pets. She shares her home with the miniature Pot-Bellied Pig "Piggy Sue", who retrieves and often entertains at the clinic. She is co-author of "The Illustrated Standard of the Pygmy Goat" and the "Rumenator."

The End